21 Days of Effective Co<!---->

Everyday Habits and Exercises to Improve Your Communication Skills and Social Intelligence

Positive Psychology Coaching Series

Copyright © 2018 by Ian Tuhovsky

Author's blog: www.mindfulnessforsuccess.com
Author's Amazon profile: amazon.com/author/iantuhovsky
Instagram profile: https://instagram.com/mindfulnessforsuccess

All rights reserved. No part of this publication may be reproduced, stored in a retrieval system, or transmitted, in any form or by any means, electronic, mechanical, photocopying, recording or otherwise without the prior written permission of the author and the publishers.

The scanning, uploading, and distribution of this book via the Internet, or via any other means, without the permission of the author is illegal and punishable by law.
Please purchase only authorized electronic editions, and do not participate in or encourage electronic piracy of copyrighted materials.

Important
The book is not intended to provide medical advice or to take the place of medical advice and treatment from your personal physician. Readers are advised to consult their own doctors or other qualified health professionals regarding the treatment of medical conditions. The author shall not be held liable or responsible for any misunderstanding or misuse of the information contained in this book. The information is not indeed to diagnose, treat or cure any disease.
It's important to remember that the author of this book is not a doctor/therapist/medical professional. Only opinions based upon his own personal experiences or research are cited. The author does not offer medical advice or prescribe any treatments. For any health or medical issues – you should be talking to your doctor first.

Please be aware that every e-book and "short read" I publish is truly written by me, with thoroughly researched content 100% of the time. Unfortunately, there's a huge number of low quality, cheaply outsourced spam titles on Kindle non-fiction market these days, created by various Internet marketing companies. **I don't tolerate these books. I want to provide you with high quality, so** if you think that one of my books/short reads can be improved in some way, please contact me at:

contact@mindfulnessforsuccess.com

I will be very happy to hear from you, because you are who I write my books for!

Introduction: Who Is This Book For? 4

Day 1: Listen 9

Day 2: Count The Number Of Times You Interrupt Other People 14

Day 3: Become An Inclusive Communicator 18

Day 4: How To Expand Your Vocabulary 22

Day 5: Swap "But" For "And," & Embrace "Yet" 26

Day 6: Watch Your Pronouns 30

Day 7: Offer A Helping Hand 34

Day 8: Practice Saying "Thank You" 38

Day 9: Stop Trying To Score Points 42

Day 10: Ask Questions That Get Results 46

Day 11: Refine Your Voice & Speaking Style 50

Day 12: Focus On Behavior, Not Character 54

Day 13: Uncover Your Communication Background 58

Day 14: Understand How Different Generations Communicate 63

Day 15: Master The Art Of Communicating Via E-mail 69

Day 16: Stop Putting Yourself Down! 73

Day 17: Ask Someone For Advice 78

Day 18: Shut Down Nosy People 82

Day 19: Put Together A Persuasive Message 86

Day 20: Improve Your Mediation Skills 90

Day 21: Drop The Clichés 95

Conclusion 97

Recommended Reading for You 101

About The Author 124

Introduction: Who Is This Book For?

Have you ever searched for something interesting to say, wondered how to make new friends, or suffered from social anxiety? You aren't alone. There are millions of other people in your shoes.[1] Heck, I used to have similar problems. These days I can talk to almost anyone and handle everyday social situations with ease. However, it's been a long journey fraught with challenges before I reached my destination.

There's no doubt about it – communication skills are vital to success. Whether you want to improve your romantic relationships, build closer bonds with your family, make your friendships stronger, or boost your career, you absolutely must polish your communication skills.

Communication should be natural – so why do we find it challenging?

All the progress the human race has enjoyed comes down to communication. Think about it. How would we have invented our first tools, raised families, built societies, and formed governments if we hadn't been able to communicate effectively? We need these vital skills to form relationships, exchange ideas, and enjoy spending time with family and friends.

Unfortunately, our life experiences often get in the way, and we start to lose touch with our natural abilities. For example, if you are bullied at school, you might come to believe that you are an intrinsically unpopular person who will never make friends. In this kind of situation, it makes sense that your social relationships will suffer.[2]

Personally, I was raised in a family of high achievers. As a result, I often felt as though any ideas I proposed were bound to be criticized. My mother says that I was a confident preschooler, but by the age of seven, I'd started to become shy.

---

[1] Stein, D.J. et al. (2017). The cross-national epidemiology of social anxiety disorder: Data from the World Mental Health Survey Initiative. *BMC Medicine, 15, 143*.

[2] Arseneault, L. (2017). The long-term impact of bullying victimization on mental health. *World Psychiatry, 16, 1*, 27-28.

My journey

During my early twenties, I really began to appreciate just how vital communication skills really are to anyone who wants a happy, well-balanced life. As a young adult I had several good friends and dated a few women, but I didn't really feel close to anyone. Sure, I could talk to my buddies and keep my girlfriends entertained, but something was missing.

I'd watch other people at parties, in class, and at bars, talking and laughing together without a care in the world. They seemed to find small talk so easy. I felt like I must be doing something wrong since communication didn't come naturally to me.

When I landed my first job out of college, the same old issues bubbled up. It wasn't that people didn't like me, but I always felt a bit distant. I was highly introverted, constantly second-guessing myself in conversation, and unsure of how to approach people I wanted to know better.

For a while, I felt a bit sorry for myself. I assumed that some people are born to be great communicators, and that it's pointless to try and practice social skills if you aren't gifted with a natural talent for conversation. Looking back now, I had so much to learn. As I discovered, you can definitely improve your skills in this area, regardless of your age or background.

My quest for personal development soon lead me down a rewarding path where I learned a huge amount about human psychology and communication. I became hooked on self-help books, academic texts, research studies, and seminars.

There isn't enough space in this introduction to list my favorite authors and communication experts. I'm proud to say that I'm now an author myself, having written several books on communication skills, social intelligence, and other aspects of self-improvement.

So far, I've helped hundreds of people improve their relationships and kick-start their careers – and I've got the reviews to prove it! If this book resonates with you, be sure to check out:

Communication Skills Training: A Practical Guide To Improving Your Social Intelligence, Presentation, Persuasion and Public Speaking

The Science of Effective Communication: Improve Your Social Skills and Small Talk, Develop Charisma and Learn How to Talk to Anyone

The Science of Interpersonal Relations: A Practical Guide to Building Healthy Relationships, Improving Your Soft Skills and Learning Effective Communication.

Making the jump from reading to action

All the self-development in the world remains useless until you are willing to put into practice everything you've learned. It takes a lot of time to research the right information, process it, and experiment with new techniques. At the start of my own journey, I desperately hunted for a book packed with brief but effective communication exercises based on sound psychological research. Alas, I couldn't find one.

Over a decade later, I have written the kind of book I wanted as a young man – you are holding it in your hands. My aim is to help people develop their skills quickly without having to spend countless hours poring over hundreds of resources.

How to use this book

This guide contains 21 communication topics, together with actionable exercises, that will give your current skills a complete overhaul. It doesn't matter whether you are naturally shy, naturally extroverted, or somewhere in the middle – the principles in this book apply to everyone.

I won't overload you with new information, but present enough material to make a positive impact on your social life in a short space of time.

You have probably already heard of the saying, "It takes 21 days to form a new habit." It won't come as a surprise to learn that I looked to this piece of popular wisdom when coming up with this book's title.

However, I've got a confession to make – 21 isn't a magic number. Contrary to popular opinion, the length of time it really takes to form a new habit varies from 18 to 254 days.[3]

That's the bad news, but there's good news, too. This 21-day challenge provides the perfect starting point for anyone who wants to hone their communication skills. You won't be able to implement a completely new set of habits in 21 days, but you'll notice a real difference as will your friends, family, and coworkers.

The book is designed to be used over the course of 21 days, but I realize that life doesn't always go as planned. Your schedule might not allow you to use the exercises in precisely the right order. That's okay – just do the best you can. I've made sure that you can change the sequence if needed.

Caution ahead.

Before we get started, I want to end this introduction with a couple of cautions. First, these challenges are just that – challenges. They are not easy. To be honest, they've been specially designed to push you beyond your comfort zone. Prepare to work hard, because the results are well worth the effort. Communication is like any other skill – the more you practice, the better you become.

On a lighter note, I'm also going to caution you that practicing and improving your communication skills can be addictive! When you start paying more attention to how

---

[3] Clear, J. (2017). *How Long Does It Actually Take To Form A New Habit?* jamesclear.com

people relate to one another on a day-to-day basis, you'll start to notice that particular patterns show up again and again.

It's been over ten years since I started taking an interest in human relationships, and there's still so much I want to learn. I hope this book sparks a similar reaction in you.

Your Free Mindfulness E-book

I really appreciate your interest in my work! Congratulations on taking another step in your journey toward self-development and proactively making your life better. As a special gift, I would love to offer you a complimentary 120-page e-book about Mindfulness-Based Stress and Anxiety Management Techniques.
It will provide you with a solid foundation to kick-start your self-development success and help you become much more relaxed, while at the same time, becoming a more focused and effective person. With easy to understand explanations, it's a useful free supplement to this book.

To download your e-book, please visit:

http://www.tinyurl.com/mindfulnessgift

Enjoy!
Thanks again for being my reader! It means a lot to me!

Day 1: Listen

Before you even think about your responses to other people, you need to sharpen your listening skills. Have you ever had a conversation with someone whose body is there, but their mind is not? Frustrating, isn't it?

Poor communicators think that "listening" is merely the act of waiting for their turn to speak all while mentally composing their response. This is a grave mistake. Listening is so much more – it's a way of providing someone else the chance to share their thoughts and ideas, to build emotional intimacy, and to show empathy.

Today, you're going to learn the basics of great listening, and then undertake an exercise that will allow you to put these tips into practice.

Listening isn't simply about giving another person the chance to vocalize what's on their mind, although this is valuable in its own right. Listening is also the first step towards personal change.

Psychotherapist Carl Rogers, one of the most influential psychologists of the 20th century, noted that when someone gives us the chance to talk about what has happened to us and how we feel about it, we start to realize the best way to change our thoughts and behaviors.[4]

Although taking advice from someone else can be useful, we are most likely to change for the better if we work through our problems out ourselves. Being able to talk freely to an understanding listener is one of the most effective ways of achieving this.

If your conversation partner rambles, or their thoughts don't seem to make sense, hold your tongue and give them the space they need. They might want to talk to several other people first before implementing a plan, or they may need to process the issue

---

[4] Rogers, C., & Farson, R.E. (1957). *Active Listening*. gordontraining.com

in their own time. Try not to get frustrated! Extend to others the patience you would like to receive in return.

Top tips that will make you an outstanding listener

1. Use non-intrusive verbal and non-verbal signals to encourage them to keep talking: Nodding, and saying, "Uh huh" and "I see" are short, unobtrusive signals that encourage further disclosure. Silence is also okay – sometimes, someone needs a few moments to get their thoughts organized before continuing the conversation. Give them space.

2. Let them keep going until they run out of steam: When I learned to listen properly, I was amazed to discover that a lot of people desperately want someone to slow down and hear what they have to say. This is especially true if they feel angry, upset, or need to work through a problem.

One of the most useful, fundamental – and difficult – listening skills of all is to keep quiet and let the other person hold the floor. If you are dealing with an angry or frustrated individual, they won't be able to think clearly until they have offloaded everything that's on their mind.

3. Do not play the role of armchair psychologist: To some extent, everyone is a psychologist. We all like to come up with our own theories about why so-and-so is so angry all the time, why our cousin always falls for men who treat her badly, etc.[5] Analyze away – on your own time.

When someone shares important information with you, do not speculate about their personal motivations, or why they behave in a particular manner. At best, you'll come across as a bit too nosy. At worst, your conversation partner will feel patronized and angry. At *you*.

---

[5] Allen, J.G. (2010). *Why everyone's an armchair psychologist.* saynotostigma.com

4. Do not interrupt with unsolicited advice: Even if you've been in the same situation or faced the same problems as someone else, do not offer your ideas or solutions unless asked for them. There are few things more annoying than unwanted advice or suggestions.

Resist the urge to tell them that you know exactly what they are going through. To put it bluntly, you don't. Two people can have a similar experience, yet their personality types, upbringing, and previous life events mean that they will not experience the same emotions.

If your conversation partner asks for your input, then go ahead – but gauge their response. If they appear open to your feedback, continue. However, if they start frowning, crossing their arms, or give any indication that your advice isn't helpful or welcome, stop and ask whether they want you to continue.

Remember, no one is obliged to follow your recommendations. Put your ego to one side. Once you have contributed, it's up to the other person to strategize their next move. Furthermore, they may not be divulging the whole story, and they will need to take other facts and considerations into account when drawing up a plan of action.

5. Re-phrase someone else's words, but don't parrot them back: You may have heard that repeating someone's words back to them shows that you have been listening. This is true – to a point. A fine line exists between reflecting understanding and quoting someone verbatim.

I'll use an example to illustrate the concept. Suppose that your friend said the following:

"I've been feeling quite lonely lately. It seems like my family doesn't care what I'm doing or whether I'm even happy."

Here are two potential replies. Which do you think would help your friend feel truly heard, and which would make them feel really annoyed?

"So, you feel like they aren't giving you much attention right now?"

Or

"You've been feeling lonely lately, and like your family doesn't care what you're doing?"

The second response shows that you heard the actual words, but it also sounds downright weird! Your friend might wonder if she's been talking to a parrot instead of a normal human being. I prefer the first response since it reflects an absorption of the meaning behind the words in addition to the words themselves.

6. Check your assumptions: We all tend to view the world through the lens of our own preferences and experiences. For example, if you are close to your parents and enjoy talking to your mother on the phone every week, you are likely to be upset on someone else's behalf if they tell you that their own mother is very ill.

But if your conversation partner happens to have a distant relationship with their parents, they probably won't expect an overly sympathetic reaction. In fact, your sympathy might make them feel uncomfortable.

What's the lesson here? Do not project your own feelings onto someone else. Let them tell you what a situation means for them personally. Under no circumstances should you tell them how to feel. Accept everyone's differences, and that no one will react in exactly the same way under the same circumstances.

Put It Into Practice.

Your challenge for today is to phone a friend or relative you haven't seen or spoken to in a while, and then use the conversation as an opportunity to practice your active listening skills.

You don't need to be on the phone for hours, just try a 20-minute catchup. Ask them what they've been doing lately and strive to listen attentively. You might be shocked to discover how often you slip into bad listening habits. Afterwards, reread this chapter and make an honest assessment of how you did.

This exercise also comes with a nice bonus. By phoning your friend or relative, you can build and improve your relationship. Recall the last time someone called you up unexpectedly and truly wanted to know how you were doing. It felt good, didn't it? You felt valued. The person you call is going to feel the same way. Maybe you could even make it a habit to phone them on a regular basis.

Day 2: Count The Number Of Times You Interrupt Other People

If you had to identify the most annoying communication habit ever, what would it be? Admittedly there are a lot of contenders, but most of us agree that being interrupted is among the most irritating. Today, you're going to examine how often you interrupt other people, and then work on giving your conversation partners the time and space they deserve.

Interrupting people is easy to do. For example, if you participate in a heated discussion, you might want to jump right in to exert your voice. If you're passionate about an idea, your enthusiasm might bubble to the surface.

But that's where the challenge lies. Even if your ideas are excellent, your conversation partner will be too annoyed to give them the attention they deserve if you interrupt. By your interruption, you're insinuating that your thoughts and ideas are more important than theirs. As you know from personal experience, interruptions derail your train of thought.

Interruptions also make someone feel disrespected.[6] If someone values you and your ideas, they will at least have the courtesy to let you finish speaking, right? You need to apply the same principle when actively listening to others.

Interrupting can completely kill your chances of developing a good relationship with someone else, and that's not an exaggeration. If they feel as though you are more interested in steamrolling over them with your personal point of view instead of getting to know them, they will start to withdraw from you.

Here's how to kick the interruption habit:

1. Set targets and give yourself rewards: Set a realistic goal and choose a small reward as a suitable incentive. For example, you could promise yourself that if you

---

[6] Scharf, R. (2015). *5 Ways to Stop Yourself from Interrupting People*. huffingtonpost.ca

make it through the day interrupting people fewer than ten times, you will pick up your favorite magazine or candy bar on the way home.[7]

2. Stick up signs: The simplest solutions can be the best! I keep a small sticky note on my computer monitor to remind me not to interrupt others. It features a sketch of a closed mouth just beneath an ear. I glance at it when I'm on the phone or webcam. It reminds me that if I strive to grow my relationships – and my business – I need to let other people speak.

3. Write down any points you want to make in advance: While you can't take notes during an unplanned conversation, you can take a list with you to a scheduled meeting. When you know that your key points are strategically bulleted on a piece of paper, it's easier to refrain from interrupting.

In formal meetings, you can also make notes of your thoughts when someone else is speaking. Once they have finished, you can then refer to your notes and ask for clarification.

4. Remember that your silence is just as influential as your voice: No one likes a showoff or a person who appears to love the sound of their own voice. On the other hand, everyone respects someone who lets other people speak and exercises caution when offering their own opinion. If the thought of keeping quiet terrifies you, consider that your interruption habit might spring from a sense of insecurity.

Some chronic interrupters feel the pressure to prove that they have thoughts of their own or even that they have earned a place in the room. Does this sound familiar? If so, your interruption habit might be more than just an annoying quirk. It might be time to examine any underlying feelings of inferiority and address them, either by yourself or with the assistance of a qualified therapist.

---

[7] Ibid.

5. Practice biting your tongue: The phrase "bite your tongue" can be taken literally here. When you feel the urge to interrupt, sandwich your tongue between your teeth. The sensation will act as a constant reminder not to butt in.

Cultural differences

The advice I've given in this chapter assumes that you, and those around you, have been raised in a culture that interprets interruptions as a sign of rudeness. Most Westerners would agree that it's good manners to let someone else finish speaking before responding.

However, it's useful to remember that there are cultural differences in how people perceive interruptions. For instance, some cultures regard interruptions and cross-talk as normal.

To give two specific examples, those of Italian descent tend to see interruptions as an acceptable way of showing interest in a topic. Meanwhile, people raised within Japanese culture often believe that it is acceptable to interrupt someone to ask for clarification.[8]

When you meet someone, who seems especially quick to interrupt, consider the possibility that there is a culture gap. It isn't appropriate to ask someone to describe their family's heritage, but just knowing that these differences exist can help you remain calm and patient.

You can bridge the gap by making an explicit request such as, "I've got something really important to say and don't want to forget anything, so if you have any questions, could you please save them for the end?"

Put It Into Practice

---

[8] Gino, F. (2017). *How to Handle Interrupting Colleagues.* hbr.org

Today's exercise is really, really simple – or at least, it's simple in theory. Count how many times you interrupt other people in all your conversations, and then use the tips above to stop yourself. Ideally, you should try to talk with at least three people. If you can do this while in a group, even better.

The first time I tried this exercise, I was dismayed to discover that I struggled to even let people finish their sentences. My intentions weren't to be rude or annoying, but my conversation partners must have been thoroughly irritated.

Unless I make an effort to keep myself in check, I still catch myself interrupting others a bit too often. It's a tough habit to break, but your friends and family will thank you for it. Who knows, you might learn something new if you master the art of keeping your mouth shut.

Day 3: Become An Inclusive Communicator

When it comes to politics and social issues, we all have our own opinions. Yet one thing most of us can agree on is that everyone, regardless of their background or individual characteristics, deserves to be treated with respect. Today, you will learn about the importance of inclusive communication.

What is "inclusive communication" anyway?

In a nutshell, a good inclusive communicator takes care not to alienate or offend an entire group of people based on their personal attributes. They do not make assumptions based on an individual's characteristics. Inclusive communication acknowledges and values diversity.

Mastering this skill is increasingly important in the 21st century. Thanks to globalization, people from all backgrounds now work and socialize together. Inclusive communication builds harmonious relationships between individuals, and it even boosts business performance. Research reflects a positive correlation between gender diversity, ethnic diversity, and profit in organizations.[9]

Tips for inclusive communication

1. Don't emphasize a characteristic if it isn't necessary to do so: For example, let's suppose that you are telling your team that an employee from another department is scheduled to work with them on a new project. This employee, a man called Sam, happens to be gay.

It would not be appropriate to say, "Sam, the gay guy from Department X, will be joining us on Monday." Sam's sexual orientation is not relevant to his work, so drawing attention to this characteristic is not necessary.

---

[9] Hunt, V., Layton, D., & Prince, S. (2015). *Why diversity matters.* mckinsey.com

2. Don't assume a person's gender or sexual orientation: Choose gender-neutral terms if possible. For example, if your manager is leaving the company and you do not yet know the gender of their replacement, it is more appropriate to use "they" in reference to the possible candidates instead of "he" or "she" until a permanent replacement is selected.

Do not assume that a person is heterosexual. It is better to use terms like "partner" or "significant other" instead of "boyfriend," "wife," and so on.

3. If you need to talk about someone's disability, do so in neutral terms: It's true that many people with disabilities do suffer as a result, but it is presumptuous to make statements such as "Peter suffers from epilepsy" or "Mary is afflicted with schizophrenia."

4. Focus on a person, not any disabilities they might have: Do not define someone by their condition or illness. For example, it is better to say, "Pat has depression" rather than "Pat is a depressive" or "Pat is depressed."

5. Do not uphold stereotypes: Making assumptions based on someone's nationality, ethnicity, or other characteristics is offensive because it shows a lack of respect for someone's individual talents and personality. This philosophy stays true even of positive stereotypes.

For example, if you meet a Chinese accountant, it would be inappropriate to suggest that Chinese people naturally make good accountants because "Asians are so good at math."

6. Show respect for race and ethnicity through proper capitalization in written communication: For instance, "Native American", "Black", and "Torres Strait Islanders", should always be capitalized. If in doubt, look up the term in a dictionary or use a reputable online resource.

7. Be mindful of context: Bear in mind that in some instances, it is acceptable for members of a group to use words that would be offensive if used by outsiders. For example, some members of the LGBT+ community refer to themselves as "queer."

However, this word is usually considered offensive if used by a heterosexual person, and not all LGBT+ people accept it in the first place. If in doubt, any "loaded" terms that have historically been used to insult or belittle others are best avoided.[10]

8. Avoid patronizing individuals or groups of people: If you have a disability, you might have heard someone describe you as "brave" or "inspiring" for carrying out normal day-to-day tasks such as cleaning your home, going to work, or exercising at the gym.

I have a cousin who walks with a cane following a car accident several years ago. Several well-meaning people have praised him for being "an inspiration". Their intentions are good, but my cousin just feels patronized. Do not assume that just because someone has a disability that they want to be recognized for merely existing!

Is inclusive communication really necessary?

I respect the fact that some people think inclusive communication is "too politically correct." However, wherever your personal views land, you can quickly find yourself in trouble if you do not use inclusive communication. For instance, using sexist language in the workplace could land you in hot water with HR, or earn you a reputation as someone who doesn't keep up with modern etiquette.

Why making offensive jokes is harmful, even if you really are "only joking"

Over the years, I've met a few people who claim that it's acceptable to make offensive jokes, or stereotype groups of people, as long as you don't really hold offensive views.

---

[10] GLAAD. (2017). *GLAAD Media Reference Guide.* glaad.org

But here's something to think about – people who *do* support negative stereotypes and hold racist, sexist or other offensive views will feel justified whenever they hear such "jokes."

This means that racism, sexism and other forms of bigotry go unchallenged.[11] Do not make jokes that rely on disparagement humor, and let others know that you don't find them funny.

Put It Into Practice

Exercise I

Do you express assumptions or stereotypes (whether positive or negative) when talking about particular groups? The next time you take part in a conversation that includes a discussion about other people, consider whether your choice of words is respectful. Could you be a more inclusive communicator? If applicable, make a note of where and how you could improve next time around.

Exercise II

Switch on the TV (or go on YouTube) and find a show that features a lot of dialogue. Watch it for 15-20 minutes. Are the people taking part in the conversation upholding any negative views or beliefs about particular groups? Do you hear similar language in your everyday interactions? If so, how could you challenge it?

---

[11] Ford, T.E. (2016). *Racist and sexist jokes aren't harmless – they can actually perpetuate discrimination.* uk.businessinsider.com

Day 4: How To Expand Your Vocabulary

You will be judged more favorably in social situations if you can demonstrate a broad vocabulary. Most people assume higher levels of education and intelligence when a person knows the meaning of many words and can use them correctly within the scope of normal conversation.

Those who understand and appreciate complex words and phrases are at a real advantage, both personally and professionally. Today, you will learn why a big vocabulary is a valuable asset, and how to add more words to your personal dictionary.

Why your vocabulary really does make a difference

There is a link between vocabulary and occupational success. A study by linguistics and education researcher Johnson O'Conner found that people who achieve high scores on vocabulary tests are significantly more likely to obtain high-level positions in the workplace.

This finding still applies when gender, age, and level of schooling are controlled.[12] Even more interesting, vocabulary test performance *predicts* success – it's not just a byproduct of working in senior positions or encountering with educated people.

So, what's going on here? In a nutshell, a strong vocabulary is the best foundation for communication, and communication is the starting point for success. When you have more words at your disposal, you are in a better position to deliver exactly the right message.

The richer your vocabulary, the more accomplished you will become in communicating nuanced ideas, and in understanding new lines of thought and reason.[13]

---

[12] Litemind. (2017). *Top 3 Reasons to Improve Your Vocabulary.* litemind.com
[13] Ibid.

Someone with a wide vocabulary can tailor their oral and written communication to a range of audiences, meaning that they can grow productive relationships with others that allow them to flourish.

A wide vocabulary also allows you to absorb information from complex sources, which provides you with the tools you need to improve your personal and professional skills. For example, if you are comfortable reading and interpreting high-level textbooks, you are more likely to benefit from advanced education and training than people who only recognize common everyday words.

When you are familiar with complex words, your reading speed will also improve, because you won't have to pause to define a word. Obvious, right?

Here are a few strategies that will help you out:

1. Use a new word every day: Get into the habit of looking up a new word each morning, and then using it at some point during the day. If it's a particularly obscure word and you can't fit it into a conversation naturally, at least tell someone that you learned a cool new word, and then tell them what it means.

2. Use apps and online games to expand your vocabulary: There are hundreds of free apps and games designed to help users learn new words. One of my favorites is Free Rice (freerice.com). It's a simple multiple-choice game that tests your vocabulary. The more questions you get right, the more difficult the questions become!

If you give an incorrect answer, the site will show you where you went wrong. As an added bonus, for every correct answer you give, the site's founders donate a small amount of rice to people in need. PowerVocab (vocabulary.com), 7 Little Words (7littlewords.com), and Words With Friends 2 (zynga.com) are all popular apps that make learning new words simple.

3. Become a word enthusiast: Learning words in isolation will help grow your vocabulary but gaining a deeper appreciation of a word's structure and roots will put you in a good position to understand new words you encounter in the future.

When you first learn a word, break it down to its constituent parts.

For example, the word "orthostatic" means "relating to or caused by an upright posture". If you break the word apart, you'll see that it's a fusion of "ortho" which means "straight", and "static" which means "concerned with bodies at rest". Learning the definitions of prefixes and suffixes will help you decipher new words.

4. Read widely: This is the classic piece of advice for anyone who wants to sound intelligent and educated. Don't stick to the same books and magazines that you normally read. Challenge yourself by exploring new topics, and by reading denser and more challenging text.

Set aside at least 15 minutes of reading time each day. In my opinion, there's no excuse not to read – not only does it improve your vocabulary, but it will also help you become a well-rounded individual capable of conversing with virtually anyone.

5. If you aren't sure what a word means, ask. It's normal to feel embarrassed when someone uses a word that you don't recognize, but it's a golden opportunity to learn something new.

If someone tries to make you feel inferior on the basis that you don't happen to know what a word means, then that's their problem. If you really can't ask at the time, at least make a note of the word and look it up later in your dictionary.

Put It Into Practice

Exercise I

Today I want you to learn five new words, and then incorporate them into your spoken or written communication.

Exercise II

Take a look at the apps and websites mentioned in this chapter and commit to using one of them for at least five minutes each day for a week.

Day 5: Swap "But" For "And," & Embrace "Yet"

Sometimes, it's the little things that make a huge difference. Today, I'm going to draw your attention to "but", "and", and "yet." The words we choose shape not only how other people see us but how we see ourselves.

When you master the art of positive communication, the world will start to appear more welcoming. You will begin seeing opportunities rather than problems, and other people will be drawn to your proactive, upbeat personality. You don't have to believe that these tips will work – just put them into practice and see the difference for yourself.

"But", "and", and positive communication

How often do you hear people say "but" statements? Here are a few examples:

"I'd love to go on vacation, *but* I'm scared of flying."

"I'd like to go back to school, *but* I don't have any free time."

"I want to run a marathon, *but* I'm so out of shape."

In each of these statements, the speaker ascribes a particular explanation to a problem or situation. They assert that *because* they are scared of flying, they can't go on vacation, or that they have no free time so they can't go to school, or that they are out of shape and therefore cannot run a marathon.

What most people don't realize is that a typical "but" statement is unnecessarily limiting and negative. This becomes more apparent if you take out "but" and then insert "and" instead. Take the first example in the list above – "I'd love to go on vacation, but I'm scared to fly."

Swap "but" for "and" and you notice the difference immediately:

"I'd love to go on vacation, *and* I'm scared to fly."

The revised version suggests that the speaker just so happens to be afraid of flying, *plus* they want to go on vacation. It's a subtle difference but it matters! It implicates that the person has a desire plus a problem to be solved, rather than a desire that will be thwarted by their problem.

When I start working with a client, I often notice that they parrot the same old "but" statements repeatedly. They become our own personal stories – excuses that we don't question. We assume that they are true and take them to heart as the gospel truth.

These intrinsic beliefs become somewhat akin to a script. The more you repeat them, the further entrenched you are in the role of someone who would love to change their life yet cannot do so because they are held back by a single factor beyond their control.

When I teach my clients to drop the "buts" and swap them for "and" instead, I usually see a rapid transformation. Within a few minutes, this mindset shift starts to show in their expression. Hope replaces desperation as they realize that the way you frame a situation makes all the difference when coming up with solutions to a challenge.

Another problem with using "but"

"But" can also make people defensive. As soon as we hear that little word, most of us assume that criticism or bad news is on the horizon.

For instance, if you were to tell someone that you understand their point *but* want to use another approach, they are likely to feel threatened and criticized. However, telling them that you understand their view *and* want to use another strategy will usually elicit a more positive response.

It implies that you value their input, even though you won't put it into action. This technique generates a sense of closeness and mutual allegiance.[14]

---

[14] Balint, J. (2014). *Use "And" instead of "But."* linkedin.com

The power of "yet"

Simply putting "yet" on the end of a negative statement can transform its meaning.

Let's look at a few examples:

"I don't know enough about this topic to pass the exam."

"I don't know enough about this topic to pass the exam *yet*."

"I can't get a girlfriend."

"I can't get a girlfriend *yet*."

"I just don't earn enough money to buy a house."

"I just don't earn enough money to buy a house *yet*."

Using "yet" signals to yourself and others that you haven't given up. You are acknowledging that things might change. You may not understand exactly how you will make these changes come to pass, but you are at least open to the possibility. It immediately transforms you into a more positive, optimistic person – at least in the eyes of others.

This technique doesn't just work in conversation. It is also effective when it comes to your own self-talk. It promotes a sense of positivity and potential, while still encouraging you to remain realistic. It acknowledges your current situation and problems but makes it clear that you are on the right track.

Put It Into Practice

There are two exercises for you to try today.

Exercise I

Whenever you catch yourself making a negative statement that includes the word "but", substitute "and" instead. Don't be surprised if your optimism turns out to be contagious.

This one little change will make you sound confident and positive. This will inspire others. If you aren't able to try this out in conversation, use it as a journaling exercise instead.

Give yourself five minutes to write down any "but" statements you've been making recently. What happens if you use "and" instead of "but"? Personally, I feel less helpless in the face of my difficulties when I make this simple swap.

Exercise II

Go on a "Yet Hunt". Whenever you make a negative statement or bemoan that you are lacking some kind of resource, stick a "yet" on the end. You could also silently add a "yet" to the end of other people's sentences and see for yourself how it changes their meaning. You might be tempted to start telling others that they'd feel better if they started using "yet" more often, but this is best avoided unless you're certain they value constructive feedback.

Day 6: Watch Your Pronouns

Unless you are reciting a monologue, you need to always consider the needs of your conversation partner. Never bore them. Break this rule at your peril. There's no point in getting your views across if no one is going to be listening to them anyway.

Do you like to talk about yourself? You're normal!

If you were to ask the average person whether they enjoy talking about themselves and listening to the sound of their own voice, they would probably say "Me? No, of course not". But let's get real – most of us love talking about ourselves. In moderation, that's perfectly okay. You are living your own life, so it's natural that you find your own experiences fascinating.

In addition, people who never reveal anything about themselves are not perceived as trustworthy. The best communicators know how to balance self-disclosure with respect for other people.

Limit your "I"s

A fascinating research study carried out in 1988 at the University of California found a link between narcissism and the number of times a person used "I" during a five-minute monologue. The subjects, 24 men and 24 women, were allowed to speak on a topic of their own choosing for several minutes.

Their monologues were recorded, and the researchers then counted the number of times each person used first person pronouns. The participants who achieved higher scores on measures of narcissism tended to use "I" more often.[15]

---

[15] Raskin, R., & Shaw, R. (1988). Narcissism and the Use of Personal Pronouns. *Personality, 56, 2,* 393-404.

So, does this mean that "I" talk is a reliable indicator of narcissism? Not quite. Later research has shown that there actually is no relationship between the two.[16] What does this mean for those of us who want to make a good impression?

Here's the important part – although psychologists disagree on whether "I" talk is really related to narcissism; the average layperson picks up on it. In other words, a psychologist might realize that "I" talk doesn't necessarily mean you are narcissistic, but most other people will.[17] In conclusion, it's safe to say that avoiding excessive "I" talk will benefit you.

When to use "I"

Too much "I" talk will not endear you to anyone, but sometimes it's the best approach. Here's when you should use it:

1. When you are being assertive: If you are standing up for your rights, using "I" draws a firm line between you and someone else, allowing you to state exactly how the situation makes you feel.

Let's suppose that your partner fails to do their fair share of the household chores. Instead of listing their faults in an aggressive manner and telling them that they need to change immediately, it would be more effective to use "I" talk to explain how their actions have made you feel.

Someone can argue with your interpretation of their actions, but they can't argue with your own feelings. "I" statements are less inflammatory than accusations beginning with "you."

---

[16] Carey, A.L., et al. (2015). Narcissism and the Use of Personal Pronouns Revisited. *Journal of Personality and Social Psychology, 109, 3,* 1-15.
[17] Ibid.

To continue with the above example, it would be better to say, "I feel undervalued when I come home to find that you have not cleaned the kitchen after you promised to do so" than "You don't do anything, and the house is a complete mess!"

2. When you want to introduce a potentially controversial opinion: If you are talking about a sensitive topic, such as religion or politics, it's a good idea to communicate to everyone listening that you can tolerate other people's opinions. Your views are your own and do not represent those of everyone else.

To avoid appearing rude, do not present your opinion as fact – preface it with an "I." Countless arguments could be prevented if only people took a second to acknowledge that not everyone feels the way they do, and that differences are okay.

3. When you want to claim credit for an idea: In most cases, it's to your advantage to work with others when coming up with a plan or new idea. You will be more popular if you are willing to work as part of a team.

However, sometimes it's better to establish that you alone deserve the credit. For example, if you are aiming for a promotion at work and your manager values self-sufficiency, use "I" when talking about your ideas.

Cut down on "I" talk, and use "we" talk instead

The word "we" instantly conjures up a feeling of solidarity. "We" talk emphasizes similarities and common experiences, which generates a sense of intimacy. You can do this in such a subtle way that no one will notice. You don't have to change the meaning of what you say. Simply make a few minor adjustments.

Look at the examples below to see how this works:

"*I* think the meeting starts at three."

"*We* have to be at the meeting room by three, right?"

"*I* remember the summer of 2012. It was really hot."

"*We* had a really hot summer in 2012."

"*I* think that house will be too expensive."

"*We* need to find out whether that house will be too expensive."

Put It Into Practice

Exercise I

Today, you are going to count the number of "I"s you use. Don't worry if you start to lose track. It's not necessary to cut "I" out completely. Just challenge yourself to remain aware of what you are saying.

Exercise II

Sit in on a conversation and monitor the number of times each party starts a sentence with "I." Keep two running tallies for a few minutes, one for each individual. Are the numbers roughly even? Do they both seem happy with the way the conversation flows?

This exercise works particularly well if you can observe two strangers, because you won't have any preconceptions about their personalities or the events they are discussing. Whenever I've tried it, I usually notice that if one person uses a lot of "I" talk, their conversation partner will start to sound bored. Bear this in mind the next time you catch yourself saying "I" too often.

Day 7: Offer A Helping Hand

Giving and receiving help is part of being human. Lending a hand to someone who needs practical or emotional support is rewarding, and it can enrich your relationship. Unfortunately, offering help isn't always simple. Today, you'll learn how to reach out to someone in need.

Why asking someone if they need help can get complicated

There is a fine line between offering someone help and making comments that imply they are incompetent. Unless you approach the issue in a sensitive way, the other party may feel patronized. They might also suspect that you are trying to meddle in their lives. On the other hand, withholding help can make you appear cold and aloof.

Here are a few tips you can use to strike the right balance:

1. When offering someone help, tell them exactly why you are reaching out: When you do this, the other person will understand that your offer is motivated by a desire to make their life easier. Make it clear that you don't want to order them around.

For example, let's suppose that your friend has recently moved into a house that requires extensive structural and cosmetic work. When you visit them in their new home, you note that the place is a complete mess. Your friend appears tired, almost on the verge of tears.

They tell you that the house is proving to be a far bigger project than they'd anticipated. You want to offer to help your friend, but you don't want to patronize them by implying that they can't possibly undertake the work alone.

Which of the following questions do you think would work best in this case?

"Do you need help with this place?"

OR

"Hey, I've noticed that you seem really tired lately, and this house is a pretty big project. I'd love to help you. Could I come over this weekend and lend a hand with the wiring?"

The latter is more sensitive, because it shows your friend that you have taken the time to understand the problem they face. It suggests that you have taken an inventory of their situation and are not just making a misguided offer of help because you think they are incapable of doing the job themselves.

2. Ask "How can I help?" or "Can I help by doing X?" instead of making a vague offer of assistance: Does the following situation sound familiar? You've had some bad news. You tell someone else about it. They say, "Just call me if you need help", or "If I can do anything, let me know".

These offers are well-meaning, but they are vague. They also sound formulaic and platitudinous. It's hard to know whether they have been made just for the sake of politeness.

What's the lesson here? If you are offering help, make your offer specific. Failing that, at least ask a question that gives the other person a chance to let you know what they need. Think about the day-to-day challenges someone in their situation might face.

For example, if your friend's child is in hospital, you might realize that shopping for groceries and keeping the house clean may seem overwhelming under the circumstances. You could ask, "Can I help by doing a grocery run?" or "Would you like me to come over and do the housework for you?".

The same principles apply in the case of minor problems. If your colleague appears overworked and stressed one morning, don't just stand there and say, "You look busy, so let me know if you need help." It would be better to say, for example, "Can I help by doing that filing for you?" or "Would you like me to take the notes for this afternoon's meeting?"

3. Focus on helping a person change their circumstances, not their character: Sometimes, a person's problems are caused by their character deficits. For instance, if your friend has lost their job because they are habitually late and tend to daydream while sitting at their desk, they have caused their own problems by failing to adhere to basic standards of behavior expected of an employee.

However, your role in this situation is not to "fix" their character, or to lecture them on how to live their life. Yes, profound personal change is possible – but it must come from the individual, and it may require professional assistance.

You could help them look for a new job or help them to research training providers if they want a change of career. It is futile to tell someone about their own faults and then expect instant change.

They probably already know what they need to work on and will not appreciate your amateur psychoanalysis. In fact, they will probably resent your attempts to interfere, and it could damage your relationship. Offer practical help or offer to listen, but never try to "help" by remodeling someone's personality.

4. Don't offer emotional help or support unless you know you can remain nonjudgmental: Offering to help someone by "talking over a problem" or "just listening" is great – if you have the right skills.

Be honest with yourself. If your friend or relative faces a huge problem, can you trust yourself to stay quiet and listen, even if they choose to do something you don't agree with? (This is especially important if their next steps could have a direct impact upon your personal life.)

If you are not able to listen, help them find someone else who can be relied upon to hear them out. Ideally, this person will not have any emotional investment in the situation.

5. Be flexible if you want to offer money: If you have a friend or relative who is in financial trouble, you might want to help out. (Assuming, of course, that you can afford it) However, many people are sensitive when it comes to the topic of money and are reluctant to accept it from friends and family. Don't be surprised if someone turns down your offer of financial aid.

If someone is too proud to accept a gift of money, or if it goes against their principles, you could either offer a loan instead (at no interest) or provide them with opportunities and services that will help them get back on their feet. For instance, you could offer to babysit their kids for free while they attend job interviews or set them up with professional contacts in your field.[18]

Put It Into Practice

Do you know someone who has been having a hard time lately? Call them up and offer your help. Make sure you know in advance what you are capable of giving and that you don't promise more than you can deliver.

---

[18] Wilde, A. (2017). *Etiquette for the Best Way to Offer Money Without Offending.* pocketsense.com

Day 8: Practice Saying "Thank You"

"Thank you" is one of the most important phrases in our language. Human relationships are built on shared interests and good communication but also on mutual acts of service. For example, close friendships are based on an agreement (usually left unspoken) that each friend will listen to the other in times of need.

Today, you are going to think about how often you give thanks to those who offer help. Even self-made men and women need a helping hand or two on their way to success.

No one likes whiny, ungrateful individuals who refuse to acknowledge their good fortune. There are few things more annoying than someone who has so many reasons to be thankful but complains all the time. Even more unpopular are those who receive help from others but rarely bother to acknowledge it.

It doesn't matter how much status you have, or even how famous you are – you are never "too good" to stop and give thanks to everyone who helps you out. It's an easy way to develop a reputation as a happy, positive individual that everyone wants to be around.

1. Build on a bare "Thank you:" A simple "Thank you" is always appreciated, but there's a quick trick that will ensure you leave a lasting impression. Using a few extra words, tell someone precisely what has filled you with gratitude.

For example, suppose a colleague has agreed to attend a meeting on your behalf and take notes because you are urgently needed on a project. Most people would take the notes and say, "Thank you so much!"

That's fine, but what do you think might happen if you were to use one of the following phrases instead?

"Thank you for taking the time to make those notes for me."

"Thank you for standing in for me and getting that information."

"Thank you for taking such detailed notes, that was so helpful of you."

These alternatives are specific and personal. This tactic will make the other person feel more appreciated for what they have done, which will enrich your relationship. It also prevents you from taking others for granted.

For example, if your partner fixes dinner most evenings, you may find that over time you stop showing a noticeable degree of appreciation. Making an effort to show how much you value them will nurture your relationship.

2. Offer to repay their kindness: If someone has gone out of their way to help you, offering them assistance in return will demonstrate your appreciation. Most people won't take you up on it, but they'll still be pleased that you asked. Ask, "How can I return the favor?" or "Is there anything I can do in return?"

You could also tell them that if there's anything they need in the future, they can call on you to help. Remember, relationships are built on give and take. In a healthy friendship, both parties are willing to give and receive support.

3. Never reject a compliment: I think most of us are occasionally guilty of brushing off a compliment or piece of praise. Even a well-timed compliment can be enough to make some of us blush with modesty but arguing with someone trying to compliment you is rude.

The only appropriate response is a sincere "Thank you" "I'm so glad you think so" or similar.

What if you suspect that someone is merely trying to flatter you, or is giving you a sarcastic compliment? You should still say "Thank you" because you'll win no matter what. If they are giving you a true compliment – you win.

If they are being sarcastic or manipulative and you say "Thank you" before changing the subject, you still win because you haven't allowed them to drag you down to their level.

Saying "Thank you" will also make you feel grateful for what you have, which in turn will make you happier. Research shows that "gratitude listing" – literally writing down what you are thankful for – improves mood and well-being. This is even true for people living with a chronic health condition.[19]

When you make a point of thanking other people, you will automatically start noticing what goes well in your life. It helps you develop a growth mindset, which encourages you to identify opportunities instead of obstacles. Unsurprisingly, research has also shown that people who are thanked for their efforts enjoy greater mental health than those who feel underappreciated.[20]

Put It Into Practice

Exercise I

Today, your challenge is to find opportunities to express thanks and gratitude. There are bound to be at least a few people to thank. Let everyone know how much their help means to you.

Even if someone just holds the door open, look them in the eye and say, "Thanks a lot!" If you are lucky enough to be on the receiving end of a significant act of kindness, let the other person know how much you appreciate them.

Exercise II

---

[19] Emmons, R.A., & McCullough, M.E. (2003). Counting Blessings Versus Burdens: An Experimental Investigation of Gratitude and Subjective Well-Being in Daily Life. *Journal of Personality and Social Psychology, 84, 2,* 377-389.

[20] Lanham, M.E., Rye, M.S., Weill, L.S., & Rimsky, S.R. (2012). How gratitude relates to burnout and job satisfaction in mental health professionals. *Journal of Mental Health Counseling, 34, 4.*

If possible, take it one step further and make time to tell a loved one how much you value their ongoing help and support. You could even call them up just to tell them how wonderful they are!

One day, I realized that I had never told my mother how much I appreciated all the support she'd given me during my college years, especially those times I struggled to stay motivated.

That night, I called to let her know how vital her love and help had been on my academic journey. I told her that although I should have made that call years ago, I figured it was better late than never. She was surprised, but then burst into happy tears. Never underestimate the power of a sincere "Thank you."

Day 9: Stop Trying To Score Points

I'll admit it, I like being right – and I'm not the only one who feels this way! We all have our own points of view, and it's gratifying when we know (or rather, think we know) best.

The trouble comes when we set out to prove the validity of our opinion just for the sake of scoring points or making someone else confess that they were in the wrong all along.

Don't be too harsh on yourself if you've ever spent hours trying to browbeat someone into accepting your perspective on an issue or situation. We've all done it. It wasn't until my mid-twenties that I gave up on the idea of "winning" every and any debate.

When I was younger, I thought that I had somehow lost, or shown myself to be weak, unless I forced my poor opponent to concede that I was "right." Half the time, I didn't even care that much about the topic under discussion. My key concern was proving how much better I was than everyone else in the room.

Looking back, I'm embarrassed for my younger self. He was so busy trying to convince everyone of his so-called intelligence that he missed out on the chance to build some good friendships and romantic relationships.

I used to wonder why my dates rarely developed into something more. It seems so obvious in hindsight! Not many women tolerate self-righteous men who enjoy telling them why their views are totally wrong.

Needless to say, a confrontational approach doesn't lay the groundwork for a good friendship or romantic relationship, and it can drive your relatives crazy, too. It's fun to have a debate every now and then, but frequent sparring is exhausting.

You know the old saying, "Sometimes, it's more important to be happy than it is to be right"? That's what I'm talking about here. Let go of the inconsequential little arguments and save your reasoning abilities for the stuff that actually matters.

Let me be clear on what I mean in this chapter. I'm not talking about those instances where you actually need to change someone's mind. For example, if your spouse wants to move to the city whereas you think it's far better for both of you to remain in the country, you would need to make a case against the move. That's common sense.

If you want other people to like you and open up to you, it's unwise to impose your views on them for the sake of winning an argument. By all means exchange opinions and ideas but watch out for that moment you make the transition between constructive conversation and petty debate.

Why point scoring is, well, pointless

Bear in mind that point scoring rarely works anyway. The harder you push someone, and the more aggressive you are in insisting that you are in the right and they are in the wrong, the more likely it is that they will start to shut down. There is a sound neurological reason for this phenomenon.

When we find ourselves in a threatening situation, our fight or flight reflex kicks into high gear. Activity levels in the parts of the brain responsible for logical thought and reasoning drop, and the areas related to conflict are triggered to act.

The result? We become less and less interested in actually evaluating the evidence someone else provides and instead concentrate on fighting back. This is why two people can be having a rational conversation one minute then a short time later be shouting and screaming at one another.

Even if you do "win" an argument, you might suffer in the long run. You can never be certain whether someone gives in because you have managed to convince them of your point of view, or they have just stopped engaging with you because they are tired of the whole situation.

Conflict can lead to resentment when there are issues left unresolved. Just because you have apparently succeeded in bulldozing your opponent doesn't mean that they are going to forget it any time soon. If you want to preserve your relationship, make sure that any important underlying issues have actually been resolved.

Tune in to your emotional state. If you feel tense, angry, or want to punch a wall, it's a safe bet that whatever comes out of your mouth isn't going to be helpful or constructive.

Another key sign that you are more interested in scoring points than having a fruitful discussion is a sudden realization that you can't even remember what started the fight in the first place – and you don't even care!

If you still aren't convinced, think how much more relaxed you'll feel if you drop the idea that you always have to have the last word. Wouldn't it be nice to know that if someone holds a view that doesn't align with your own, you are under no obligation to start dissecting everything they say?

If you crave the excitement of a fiery argument, then why not join a philosophy discussion group or debating society? Choose a more constructive outlet for your dramatic nature. Don't let it ruin your relationships.

Put It Into Practice

Today, you are going to let other people be wrong. If you have to spend time with someone who holds views different to your own, this will be a challenge – but that's the whole point.

You are not going to waste your time and breath telling them why their opinion is null and void. Where has that gotten you in the past? Nowhere, probably. What does point scoring do for your relationships? Nothing!

If you have to excuse yourself from a situation to avoid an argument, then so be it – but try and tough it out. This exercise will show you that the world doesn't cave in when other people see things in a different way.

You'll soon learn that there is enough room in the world for opinions of all kinds. No one has a moral obligation to agree with you. You don't have a duty to convince them of your views either.

Day 10: Ask Questions That Get Results

When you need to uncover information fast, what do you do? Ask questions, of course! It should be so simple, shouldn't it? Unfortunately, as you know, it's not always easy to get clear answers from other people.

You can't force anyone to answer you, but you can greatly increase your chance of a good result by refining the way you ask questions.

Here's how to get answers:

1. Build up gently to high-pressure questions. No one likes having an important question sprung upon them. Show some empathy for their position. For example, let's say that you want to ask your manager some questions about your chances of receiving a raise next year.

Rather than charging in and asking immediately whether you think your salary will receive a boost, ask them whether it's a good time to talk about your position at the company and prospects for the future.

2. Decide whether an open or closed question is better. We're often told that asking open questions – those beginning with "Why" and "How" – is a better approach than asking closed questions that can be answered with a "Yes" or "No."

It's true that the former will yield more in-depth responses, but this isn't always a good thing. For instance, if you are talking to someone who is renowned for rambling on without getting to the point, it might be best to use a closed question instead.

3. Use a four-part structure when helping someone deal with a problem. Questions don't just help you obtain information. They are also a good way of helping someone through a crisis.

Empathy and sympathy will only take you so far. Asking the right questions will help someone come up with a plan of action that gets to the root of the problem.

Executive coach Irene Leonard recommends taking a four-step approach:[21]

A. Ask someone questions that will help them hone in on their issue. "What seems to be the issue here?" is a good starting point.

B. Obtain further information. Once you have established the underlying cause of their distress, you can then use prompts to get the full story, if necessary. Questions like "Can you tell me more about that?" and "What else can you tell me?" are useful in this context.

C. Ask them questions that establish their ideal outcome. Specifically, encourage them to tell you what a successful resolution would look like. Ask them what they want to happen, what their priorities are, and their preferred way of solving the problem. For instance, do they want to figure things out alone, with a friend, or with the assistance of a third party?

D. Ask them questions that help them pin down their next steps. For instance, you could ask them whether they have any firm ideas with regards to how they plan to proceed and how they will know when they have met their objectives.

4. Don't lead people to a particular answer. If you want to know what someone really thinks of an idea, you need to ask your question in a neutral way. In other words, you need to avoid asking leading questions. Think about how you phrase them.

Here are three examples of terrible questions that encourage an individual to give a particular kind of answer:

"Does everyone agree that we should streamline the department?"

"Don't you think that we should spend Thanksgiving at Peter's house this year?"

---

[21] Leonard, I. (n.d.). *The Art of Effective Questioning: Asking the right question for the desired result.* coachingforchange.com

"Shouldn't we put this into action as soon as possible?"

If you asked these questions, you'd be making your own biases plain. If someone disagreed strongly, they may raise objections, but most people like an easy life. Consequently, open questions can encourage poor decision-making at both home and work, which can be disastrous.

This is even more likely if you have a strong personality, because not many people will be willing to tackle your assumptions and challenge your thinking.

Let's look at a better way to ask those questions:

"What does everyone think we should do with regards to the department's structure?"

"Where do you think we should spend Thanksgiving this year?"

"When do you think we should put this plan into action?"

5. Don't force people to pick between two or three options. This approach assumes that you have already thought of all the available options. There might be viable alternatives, but you will never know if you ask questions in this format.

It's more effective to simply ask someone for their suggestions, or open with a broad statement like, "How would you handle this situation?"[22]

6. Prepare for the unexpected. Never assume that you know in advance what someone is going to say. Give them your full attention and be ready with a few phrases you can use if they share some shocking information.

"Thank you for telling me – I need time to process that," "This is a surprise, can I have a minute to take that on board?" and "I'll admit this has shocked me a little, but I'd like to talk about it further," can all help smooth over an awkward situation.

---

[22] Haden, J. (2014). *5 Ways to Ask the Perfect Question.* inc.com

There's even more advice on the art of asking questions in my book *The Science of Effective Communication: Improve Your Social Skills and Small Talk, Develop Charisma and Learn How to Talk to Anyone*.

Put It Into Practice

Today, you are going to put the above principles into practice when asking questions. If you have been meaning to get some clarification on an issue for a while and haven't gotten around to it, now is the perfect time! These questions don't have to be of great significance.

The objective is to practice getting the information you need and to have a positive conversation at the same time. Remember to put your listening skills to good use whenever the other person provides an answer.

Day 11: Refine Your Voice & Speaking Style

It's not just what you say but how you say it. Speaking at a suitable volume and pitch will make other people more inclined to listen to you. We all know people who aren't especially brilliant or interesting but still know how to engage a crowd.

These folks use their voices to grab their audience's attention. You should do likewise. It's not just actors and singers who can develop their voices. Anyone who wants to leave a positive impression should learn how to make the most of their vocal cords.

Today, you are going to discover your personal vocal range, and fix some of the most common speaking mistakes everyone makes from time to time. It doesn't matter how fascinating your message, it won't get through if no one is listening. A dull, monotonous voice will kill your communication dead.

Here's how to make your voice more exciting and easier on the ear:

1. Lower the pitch of your voice. Research has demonstrated that people who speak in a low pitch are perceived as more confident and competent than those who talk in a breathy voice. This applies to both men and women.[23] Like it or not, people can and will judge you based of your speaking voice.

Practice sitting and standing up straight, taking deep breaths, and then counting slowly from one to five as you exhale. You can also experiment with pitch by repeating the same word or sound (such as "No") at various intervals.

It's a good idea to learn how to breathe properly, regardless of whether you are seriously interested in developing a good speaking voice.

I know what you're thinking – doesn't everyone know how to breathe? Unfortunately, this isn't the case. Most of us breathe from our chests, not our diaphragms. Taking up

---

[23] Garber, M. (2012). *Why We Prefer Masculine Voices (Even in Women)*. theatlantic.com

yoga and breath-based meditation practices will help relax your muscles and ensure a consistent flow of oxygen around the body, which is great for your health.[24]

2. Use vocal exercises to develop a smoother voice. If your voice tends to quiver, particularly when you are under stress, you need to practice keeping it smooth and stable.

Take a deep breath in, then exhale at a steady rate while making a hissing sound. Repeat this several times. Tongue twisters also help you practice speaking in an even tone – try saying "three free throws," "strange strategic statistics," or another difficult phrase repeatedly until it becomes easy. Repeat these exercises a few times per day.[25]

Here's another exercise that will help you develop a sharper, cleaner voice. Moving up and down your vocal range say, "ney, ney, ney, ney, ney" ten times over. Repeat this exercise daily.[26]

3. Cut out any verbal tics. I used to say "um" a lot. At the time, I knew that I didn't sound as confident as I would have liked, but I had no idea that it was so noticeable until a friend kindly pointed it out. I was embarrassed at the time, but she helped me realize that if I wanted to be taken seriously, I'd have to work on eliminating my verbal tic!

Aside from "um," other frequent offenders include "er," "like," "yuh," and "y'know." They are okay in moderation, but if you use them repeatedly, your listeners will assume that you aren't really sure what you are talking about. If you happen to have any video or audio recordings of yourself lying around, watch or listen to them.

Count the number of times you use the words and phrases listed above. The results might surprise you, but they will spur you to action. If you don't have any material to work with, ask a friend to make a discreet recording when you are distracted.

---

[24] Ni, P. (2014). *How to Strengthen & Improve the Sound of Your Speaking Voice.* psychologytoday.com
[25] Peters, K. (2010). *Pump Up Your Speaking Voice with a Strength Training Workout.* sixminutes.dlugan.com
[26] Ibid.

5. Stick to short sentences and choose short words where possible. Whatever the education level of your audience, they will find short sentences easier to digest. Use technical terms if necessary but pick short words if it's practical to do so. Ideally, you should speak in sentences that you can get through on a single breath.[27]

6. Master the art of the pause. Effective speakers know that pauses lend extra weight to their message. For example, a brief pause between two points provides your audience with a chance to appreciate their importance. Pausing after a rhetorical question will give them a moment in which to consider the broader point you are making.

7. Vary the pitch and tone of your voice. Keeping your voice relatively low will make you sound more authoritative. However, speaking in a monotone will just bore everyone around you. Let yourself express some emotion. For example, it's fine to raise your voice in surprise or to adopt a softer tone when comforting a friend.

Put It Into Practice

Today, I'm assigning you two challenges.

Exercise I

Make sure you have at least ten minutes to yourself, or else those around you might assume you've gone crazy. Find an article or book and read it aloud for a minute. Record yourself speaking, then listen to it.

Pay attention to your volume and pitch. We don't tend to really listen to the sound of our own voices, so you may be in for a shock the first time you play it back!

Appraise your voice. Do you speak softly, loudly, or somewhere in between? Are you high-pitched, low-pitched, or "average"? Using your recorder, experiment until you

---

[27] Vanderkam, L. (2016). *How To Make Your Voice Sound Better So People Will Actually Listen To You.* fastcompany.com

know how it feels to speak in a steady, even voice at a relatively low pitch. Try the vocal exercises outlined above.

Exercise II

The second challenge is to practice speaking in a different tone of voice when in conversation. If you already know the other person, don't change your tone completely - they will just want to know why you suddenly sound completely different. Most of us can't help but respond differently to voices of varying pitches and inflections. You may be surprised at how everyone around you reacts.

Day 12: Focus On Behavior, Not Character

Today's challenge won't just improve your communication skills, it'll also give your social intelligence a boost. You're going to learn a simple trick that will help you resolve arguments, get your needs met in a relationship, and stay on everyone's good side.

Do you happen to know someone who seems popular with everyone, yet at the same time refuses to sugarcoat the truth? These folks have the ability to give criticism without making enemies and to patch up any disagreements within minutes.

I had a boss like this a few years ago. Everyone respected him. He had a reputation as a straight shooter and could be a bit blunt sometimes, but he was pretty popular. I'd watch him carefully in meetings, trying to work out how he got the balance right. He was calm and polite, but I sensed there was more to it than that.

One day, I worked up the nerve to ask him for a few tips. I had recently moved into a management position and was trying to learn how to call out unacceptable behavior in my team without earning myself a reputation as a mean or harsh boss.

"Ah," he said. "One rule. Focus on their behavior, not their character." I asked him for an example. "Well," he went on, "Last week I had to write someone up for wasting a lot of time on social media when he should have been working on a big project. He was being lazy. But I never used the word lazy and I never implied that he was wasting time."

"Instead, I talked about the facts. I explained why his conduct was inappropriate. I talked about the exact number of hours that he'd been spending online, and I actually had a printed copy of his contract on the table during our meeting. It clearly stated that he was not allowed to use company networks for personal communication. He agreed he'd messed up, and that was pretty much the end of it."

In hindsight, it sounded so obvious. My boss didn't assassinate anyone's character. All he did was take a moment to gather his evidence and ascertain the facts. He focused on what someone had actually done rather than their personality or attitude in general.

He spelled out the consequences someone would face if they didn't change their behavior, but he never took the opportunity to rip someone apart.

This doesn't just work in professional settings. Use it whenever you need to call someone out on their behavior. It's an awesome technique because it stops people from getting defensive.[28]

If you start analyzing their personality and passing harsh judgements on their character, you will find yourself drawn into an argument about what they are "really" like. This is a total waste of time and will harm the relationship.

Let's take a look at two examples that show the value in emphasizing actions and consequences instead of personality and threats.

Example 1: Your teenage son's room is a mess. You want him to clean it up.

Don't say: "Your room is a total mess. I can't believe how lazy you are. You'd better get it straightened up right now, or you'll be in trouble!"

Instead, you could say: "Your room is messy and needs a cleaning. This is my home, and you must respect that. I expect you to have cleaned it by the weekend, or you will not be allowed to use the car on Friday night."

Example 2: You are a manager. A member of your team has been late three mornings over the past two weeks, and you want them to start turning up for work on time.

Don't say: "You obviously don't care about your job, and you are letting the team down. Start getting here on time!"

---

[28] Henshaw, J. (2010). *The Secret to Giving Constructive Criticism – The Focus on Behaviors.* managing-employee-performance.com

Instead, you could say: "You have been late three times over the past fourteen days. As you know, it is important for the sake of the team's performance that everyone is here on time. If you are late again, you will receive a written warning."

By the way, this doesn't have to be a conversation about a serious, life-altering event. For example, let's suppose that a friend asks you out for dinner but then asks you to pay for everything.

They promise that they will pay you back once payday comes around, but then they don't make contact. This leaves you feeling hurt and underappreciated. You might be thinking, "So-and-so is really selfish! They always take people for granted!"

However, using the approach outlined in this chapter, you'd talk only about their actions. Telling them that you think they are a selfish leech might be satisfying for a few seconds, but is it going to help your friendship?

Nope! Stick to the facts. If you have to make a request (in this case, for your money), keep calm. Focus on what you want, why you need it, and the time frame in which you expect it to happen.

Finally, there's another advantage to this technique. When you talk about someone's behavior as opposed to their character, you are signaling that it's what they do, rather than who they are, that matters.

This can encourage them to try harder in the future, especially, if you also take care to compliment them on everything they have done right.[29] Whether they admit it or not, most people thrive on praise. Positive acknowledgement always goes down well.

Put It Into Practice

---

[29] Ibid.

Today, you are going to have a conversation with someone who has recently hurt or inconvenienced you. This serves two purposes. First, it will help clear the air and get your relationship back on track.

Second, it will give you the opportunity to practice talking about a problem in terms of someone's actions. You are not going to make character judgments, create drama, or drag up the past just for the sake of hurting them.

Day 13: Uncover Your Communication Background

You have control over your communication style. If I didn't believe that we all have the potential to become better communicators, I wouldn't have bothered writing this book!

However, there's no getting around the fact that the way you were raised has affected the way you talk to others and how you conduct yourself in relationships. It's human nature.

We are wired to imitate our parents, (or whoever was in charge of our well-being), because they were our first role models. Sigmund Freud held a lot of weird ideas, but he was right when he said that our early years play a key role in shaping our adult personalities.[30]

I believe that self-knowledge – plus action, of course – is a solid foundation for change. It can help you work your way around blocks or personal resistance. For example, you might realize that it makes sense to expand your vocabulary or talk in a more confident manner, because doing so improves your relationships and social standing. However, you may feel as though something is holding you back.

In these cases, it's a good idea to dig a little deeper and think about your underlying beliefs about who you are and how you "should" communicate affect you. For instance, if your parents taught you that others will see you as arrogant or "overbearing" when you are confident, it shouldn't come as a surprise when you feel a resistance to change.

The Story Of Jenny

Let me tell you about a client of mine. Jenny was in her mid-thirties, a successful lawyer who had been told by her work mentor that she was well on the way to being made a partner at her firm.

---

[30] Journal Psyche. (n.d.) *The Freudian Theory of Personality.* journalpsyche.org

The problem? Her mentor advised her that her promotion was unlikely to happen until she learned to become "more assertive" with the firm's biggest clients. Jenny had read books on assertiveness and even attended a seminar, but she still lacked the kind of confidence that would take her career to the next level.

"I don't get it," Jenny said in our first session together. "I know what I need to do, but something inside me just freezes up when I need to stand up for myself or argue against someone with a lot of power. Why can't I put what I learned in the seminar into practice?"

At the time, I was starting to delve into developmental psychology and felt inspired to tackle the problem from another angle. "If you don't mind," I said, "could you tell me about how your parents used to communicate with you?"

Our conversation then went like this:

JENNY: Normally, I suppose. You know, whatever "normal" means. They were pretty patient most of the time. Occasionally, my father lost his temper. Sometimes my mother would sulk if she couldn't get her way. Both of them had their own friends. Their social skills are okay.

ME: Alright. Would you say they were assertive people?

JENNY: No...yes? My father was quite assertive. If someone annoyed him, he'd always tell them. But my mother seemed to think...well, she didn't say so, but....

ME: But....?

JENNY: She didn't seem to think girls should cause anyone any bother, if you see what I mean. She never told me that women shouldn't be assertive, but now that I think about it, all her friends are the passive-aggressive type. I don't think she approves of strong women. She always praised me most when I was entertaining myself or being "nice and quiet".

As we talked further, it became apparent that Jenny's mother modeled a passive-aggressive communication style.

Jenny told me that her mother's sister had been much more straightforward and transparent, but unfortunately her aunt lived far away and was not available as a role model. Her mother was the only consistent female figure in her life, so she was the one who taught Jenny how to communicate with others.

If Jenny's father had been her primary caregiver, she would probably have learned to use a more assertive communication style. Social Learning Theory predicts that we adopt the behaviors and attitudes of the adults we spend the most time with.[31]

In this case, Jenny's mother was her main caregiver, so it was always more likely that Jenny would imitate her.

No wonder Jenny felt awkward when she tried to be assertive – it went against her early "training." The good news is that Jenny realized that she didn't have to be a replica of her mother. Once she figured out why she felt so uncomfortable when speaking up for herself, the answer motivated her to forge her own communication style.

I encouraged her to watch a couple of more assertive female lawyers in her firm and use them as new behavioral models. A few months after we started working together, Jenny got her promotion.

A few questions to ask yourself

Imagine that you and I are sitting in a coaching session right now. This is a list of the questions I'd ask you. Take your time when thinking about your answers; they can help you understand the lessons you've carried into your adult relationships.

---

[31] McLeod, S. (2016). *Bandura – Social Learning Theory.* simplypsychology.org

1. Did my parents have solid social skills? It's simple – if your parents knew how to create healthy relationships with others and sustain a good conversation, you probably picked up these skills. If not, you probably find social situations a bit confusing. This can cause you to doubt yourself and to feel shy around new people.

2. Did my parents have friends? While it's natural to prefer a larger or smaller social circle, it isn't normal to be completely friendless. If your parents never showed interest in other people, you may be confused by the rules of normal social interaction and might not know how to respond when other people show an interest in you.

3. Did my parents pass on any "rules" when it came to communication or relationships? As the case of Jenny proves, our parents' communication rulebook can come to be a defining factor in our social lives. These "rules" don't even have to be stated upfront.

Children pay more attention to what adults *do* than what they say. If it's a toss-up between learning from words or learning from actions, it's the actions that carry more weight every time.

4. Did my parents show me how to make up after an argument, or settle a difference of opinion? Disagreements are inevitable in any close relationship. If we don't understand how to understand someone's point of view, or how to reconcile following a fight, any kind of dispute will feel frightening.

5. Did my parents encourage me to express myself? I've worked with a lot of clients who don't even have the vocabulary to say how they feel. Obviously, this means they run into trouble in their relationships, because they don't have the ability to communicate with other people in an honest, authentic manner.

These clients were usually raised by parents who reacted badly to any display of strong emotion, even enthusiasm. They sent their children a clear message: It's inappropriate to express yourself.

Put It Into Practice

Today, you are going to do a bit of introspection. You don't have to write a lengthy journal entry or subject yourself to hours of analysis, but you might come up with some useful insights.

Take a piece of paper and divide it into two columns. At the top of each, write down the name of your two most important caregivers from early childhood. For most people, this will be "Mom" and "Dad," but you might have been cared for by another relative or even friends of the family.

Now, think about their communication styles. What did you learn from each of these individuals? Write down the beliefs they passed on to you. Do you want to hold on to these beliefs, or is it time to swap them for better, healthier ways of communicating?

Day 14: Understand How Different Generations Communicate

You've probably heard the old cliché, "Men are from Mars, women are from Venus." There are thousands of books and articles out there about sex differences and why men and women often misunderstand each other.

But what about age differences? We don't tend to talk about the challenges that come with communicating with people from other generations. In this chapter, you'll learn more about these differences, and how you can adjust your approach depending on your audience.

I'm going to focus on communication in the workplace, but this information is also useful when it comes to understanding generational differences in general.

Before we go any further, I want to make it clear that everyone has their own personality and preferred communication style. It's not a good idea to assume that just because someone was born in a particular era that they will behave in a certain way.

On the other hand, there are plenty of academic researchers who believe that our approach to work and relationships is partly influenced by when we were born.

The Generations You'll Meet At Work – And How To Communicate With Them

1. Baby Boomers (Born between 1946-1964): These workers triggered a revolution. When they entered the workplace, women and ethnic minorities were gradually starting to take on roles that had usually been occupied by white men. They have a proactive attitude, are competitive, and value their work as much as their family life. [32]

They came of age during a time of social change, and they tend to distrust authority. This isn't to say that they cannot work well with managers; just that they question

---

[32] Kane, S. (2017). *Baby Boomers In The Workplace.* thebalance.com

power and believe that those in management positions should have to work for their status. They don't have time for aloof, arrogant bosses. They prefer to work for people who try to understand everyone's point of view before deciding, rather than pull rank.

Some are skeptical of modern working practices such as remote working and flexible hours. In this respect, they are quite traditional.

Many are workaholics who believe that workplace competition is healthy and that loyalty to a company should be rewarded. They like teamwork and tend to believe that meetings are a productive use of their time.[33]

Communication tips: A typical Boomer will appreciate a detailed explanation of how their contribution is making a difference to the company's bottom line. They appreciate regular recognition, particularly if they devoted many years of their life to an organization. For this reason, they place more value on titles than their younger coworkers.

They came of age in an era where face-to-face communication was highly valued. If you have something of importance to say to a Boomer, schedule an in-person meeting. Most are perfectly capable of using e-mail and other modern technologies, but they were raised to value face-to-face conversations.

Boomers are not usually enthused by the idea of regular performance reviews or ongoing feedback. As far as they are concerned, they can do their jobs and appreciate the space in which to get their tasks done.

It may be necessary to explain to a Boomer that even the most competent of people can benefit from ongoing feedback, and that regular reviews do not imply that their managers believe them to be incompetent.

2. Generation X (Born between 1965-1980): More entrepreneurial than their Baby Boomer predecessors, Gen Xers grew up in relatively insecure financial

---

[33] Hammill, G. (2005). *Mixing and Managing Four Generations of Employees.* fdu.edu

circumstances with fewer economic opportunities. Compared with Boomers, they are more likely to prioritize a work-life balance, and to value independence.

They are not especially concerned with remaining loyal to an employer.[34] On the whole, they are more skeptical about life and the workplace in general than their parents and lack the optimism and appetite for change that characterized the Boomer generation. They are more comfortable using modern technology.

When it comes to authority, Generation Xers respect leaders who use a confrontational management style. Compared to Boomers, they are more comfortable asking and answering difficult questions in the workplace.

Being more willing to switch jobs and careers rather than remaining loyal to one employer for decades, they are not so concerned with keeping the peace at work. They place more emphasis on personal freedom, and many aspire to work for themselves.

Communication tips: Gen Xers like regular feedback and appreciate prompt comments and constructive criticism. They want to discover their own strengths and weaknesses and enjoy planning out their careers.

They believe that successful people are lifelong learners. They are creative, often embrace change, and appreciate the opportunity to air their opinions.

They do not place so much value on face-to-face communication as the previous generation, but their favored style could best be described as "direct". When talking to a Gen Xer, it's best to get straight to the point. They do not have as much tolerance for meetings as the Boomer generation.

3. Generation Y (Born between 1981-1997): Also known as "Millennials," this generation was the first to grow up with reliable access to computers and the internet. Compared with previous generations, they are happier to multitask, to get involved

---

[34] Kane, S. (2017). *The Common Characteristics Of Generation X Professionals.* thebalance.com

with multiple projects, and to take a flexible approach to work if the situation demands it.

For instance, the average Gen Yer will be glad to be seconded to another department or asked to apply their skills to a new area. They see work as a route to personal fulfilment and think that it's acceptable to change jobs and careers often to pursue their happiness.[35]

Members of this group are accustomed to digital rather than in person communication. They like frequent feedback, and they favor leaders who invite them to give their opinions at each stage of a project. A Gen Yer may well be ambitious, but they believe that a good work-life balance is important.

Communication tips: This group assumes that e-mails, instant messages, and even social media are perfectly appropriate mediums for workplace communication.

For a Gen Yer, writing an e-mail instead of making a phone call is not a sign of disrespect – it's just the norm for their generation. This group also likes to have answers quickly. If you keep them waiting, they are liable to become annoyed.

Always play it straight with a Gen Yer. If you can't give them feedback immediately, give them a realistic time frame and then stick to it. They are not entitled by nature – they have just grown up in a world full of information that is available day and night.

They are fully capable of recognizing authority and complying with workplace rules, but they will want to know how decisions are made and why.

4. Generation Z (Born from 1998 onwards):[36] These people have grown up in a period of increased social justice ideas and movements, and they tend to place more value on inclusive communication. For example, they care passionately about

---

[35] White, G.B. (2015). *Millennials In Search Of A Different Kind Of Career.* theatlantic.com
[36] Clark, J. (2017). *Generation Z: Are We Ready For The New Workforce?* entrepreneur.com

transgender rights, overcoming sexism in the workplace, and other social justice issues such as racism and income inequality.[37]

They have come of age in a digital culture, and are comfortable with the idea of working remotely, working online, and working for a diverse range of clients and companies. They are unlikely to work for the same boss over a long period of time.

Gen Zers are aware of the privacy and security risks that come with technology. They love social media and cannot fathom life without smartphones, but they know that everything you post online lives forever.

Thanks to increased globalization and easy access to information, they are more aware of their career options than previous generations. They value independence, innovation, and creativity. They grew up during a time of economic recession, so they are keen to earn a steady wage.

Communication tips: Inclusive communication is a good idea regardless of your audience, but it's particularly important when dealing with Gen Zers.

They are the most diverse workforce America has ever seen. Specifically, over 50% of under-18s will be of a minority ethnic group or race by 2020, and company communication policies need to respect this fact.

Gen Zers are eager to learn and they like to be asked for their opinions. In many respects, they are similar to Millennials, but they are likely to appreciate anonymous communication and to take more care when managing their online reputation. If a topic is particularly sensitive, they might prefer to meet in person so that no trace of the conversation is left online.

Put It Into Practice

---

[37] Fast Company. (2017). *If You Want To Know What Matters To Gen Z, Just Ask Them.* fastcompany.com

Think about the people you work with, or the people in your social circle, who are from a different generation. Do you feel equally at ease with people much older or younger than yourself?

Pick someone from another generation that you have struggled to connect with in the past. Having read this chapter, do you think that age differences might contribute to the problem?

If so, your task today is to try relating to this person in a new way. Your next steps will depend on the situation. I'll give you an example. Let's say that you are working on a project with two Boomers and one Gen Xer. The Boomers are happy to meet every Monday, report on their progress, then return the following week with another update.

However, the Gen Xer seems to feel as though the group isn't offering them enough guidance. Bearing in mind that Gen Xers tend to value ongoing feedback, you might decide to check in with them every couple of days instead. This would show respect for their preferred communication styles and result in more harmonious work relationships.

Day 15: Master The Art Of Communicating Via E-mail

Almost everyone uses e-mail and social media nowadays, both for professional and personal purposes. It's easy, free, and allows lots of room for creative expression.

However, you need to be careful. Text-based messages can be misinterpreted, sometimes with devastating consequences. If you are sending e-mails on behalf of a company, you could end up in a lot of trouble if they cause any offense.

Here's a shocking statistic: We misjudge the tone and meaning of the e-mails we receive up to 50% of the time. Worse, most of us believe that we can accurately figure out a sender's underlying message.[38] In this section, you'll learn how to get the tone right every time.

Here are the basic rules of writing effective e-mails that will get your message across:

1. If the other person is in a senior position, mirror their tone: If your boss opens and closes with a few formal words, you should do the same. If they start signing off with a simple "Yours," or "Regards," feel free to follow their lead. Otherwise, assume that you should use formal business language.

2. Make it easy for the recipient to clarify any points raised: If you are contacting someone about a complex issue, or you need to share a lot of information, provide them with some other means of getting back to you.

This is especially important if you are working on a time-sensitive document or project. If any new developments come to light, how can they contact you? Make sure they have your phone number as well as your e-mail address.

3. Don't fire off requests, and don't launch into a lengthy series of bullet points: Keep e-mails efficient and concise, but don't be too cold. For instance, don't

---

[38] Winerman, L. (2006). *E-mails and egos*. apa.org

send one or two-line e-mails that contain a stark request or statement like "I need this task to be done today" or "You will need to rearrange your schedule to fit this in."[39]

If you were talking to someone face-to-face, your tone of voice and body language can stand in for niceties like "Please" and "Thanks." Unfortunately, when you only have words on a screen, you need to (literally) spell them out.

Stark, request-based e-mails make the recipient feel defensive, as though they have been given an order by a demanding drill sergeant. Even if you are the boss and your subordinate has an obligation to follow your requests, it will benefit your relationship if you make the effort to sound friendly.

Punctuation also helps. Exclamation points denote yelling so be sure to use them only when conveying extreme excitement or upset. There is a big difference between "I'll see you this Friday" and "I'll see you this Friday!" As well as an e-mail saying, "Your work on that important project could use improvement!" and "Your work on that important project could use improvement." Which version would you rather receive from your superior?

4. Keep your subject line to a few words: If you can't think of a concise subject line, there's a chance that you've tried to fit too much information into one e-mail. Think about the true purpose of your message and rewrite it if necessary.

The average businessperson gets over 100 e-mails every day.[40] Make it easy for them to pick out the key points of your message.

5. Imagine that they are reading the message over your shoulder: If you aren't sure whether you've made an inappropriate remark, reread the message while imagining that they are in the room with you.

---

[39] Chartrand, J. (2011). *How To Avoid Harsh-Sounding Emails*. menwithpens.ca
[40] Held, M. (2014). *Five Ways To Keep Your Tone In Check When Writing Business Emails*. huffingtonpost.ca

Only click "Send" if you'd be happy to say it to their face. It's possible to insult someone to their face with no witnesses present but e-mail lasts forever.

6. Explain your attachments: If you need to attach a document, make sure that you reference it in the body of your e-mail. Give your attachment a relevant title that identifies it as a safe document that can be opened without risk to the recipient.

7. Use a template: Some of us don't like writing and others don't have time to craft a well-written message. Why not gather together a few templates and keep them at hand? There are plenty of free resources online.

For example, ThriveHive (thrivehive.com) offers 13 templates for small businesses[41] and The Muse (themuse.com) has compiled 27 pre-written templates that can be used in a range of business situations.[42] Why waste time working on the structure of a message when other people have already done the heavy lifting?

You can also compile your own templates. If you have written an especially fine e-mail, why not strip out the personal content and use the structure again in the future?

You can also use e-mails that other people have sent you for this purpose. However, be sure to remove all identifying information!

8. Begin or end the message with a humorous disclaimer:[43] If you are feeling especially pressured, tired, or angry when writing an e-mail and worry that the recipient will pick up on your negativity, type a quick disclaimer like "I've had a crazy week, but rest assured that I'm really looking forward to working with you!" or "In case I seem a bit sluggish this morning, it's because I've only had one cup of coffee so far!"

---

[41] ThriveHive. (2016). *13 Small Business E-mail Examples and Templates.* thrivehive.com
[42] The Muse. (n.d.) *27 Pre-Written Templates For Your Toughest Work E-mails.* themuse.com
[43] Ibid.

9. Where possible, use "Thanks in advance" to close an e-mail: Given that e-mail is a key business tool, you won't be surprised to learn that researchers have invested a lot of time into figuring out the words and phrases that get results.

Boomerang, a company that specializes in helping people manage their e-mail and improving their productivity, ran a study in which they looked at over 350,000 e-mails. The phrase "Thanks in advance" yielded a response rate of 65% according to their findings, outshining all other common sign-offs.[44]

10. Keep it simple: Unless you know the other party well, you should write using language that could be understood by a third-grader.

If you enjoy reading and writing, you might forget that most people don't actually do much of either outside of work. Using straightforward language and short sentences also reduces the risk of cross-cultural misunderstandings.

11. Don't use emojis in formal situations: This should really go without saying, but just in case it isn't obvious – do not use emojis in formal business e-mails. Save them for colleagues you know well and silly conversations with your friends. The same applies for GIFs and novelty filters on photo attachments.

Put It Into Practice

There's a good chance that you'll have to send an e-mail today. Read it aloud before you press "Send." You may discover that you haven't got the tone quite right and that it needs rewriting.

---

[44] Dizik, A. (2017). *How to avoid writing irritating emails.* bbc.com

Day 16: Stop Putting Yourself Down!

Do you tend to dismiss your own achievements? Do you tell people that you can't do X, Y, or Z, even though you managed it on previous occasions? Perhaps you even go so far as to insult yourself at every turn?

Everyone experiences moments of low confidence, and no one goes through life without at least a little self-doubt. It's healthy to take a step back sometimes and identify areas for improvement.

However, there's a big difference between staying grounded and beating yourself up in public. Today, you're going to learn why putting yourself down is a toxic communication habit that is harming your relationships, your happiness, and your chances of success at work.

Why do we put ourselves down in the first place? Well, there are a few reasons:

1. We don't want to be arrogant: This is the big one. Some of us believe that self-criticism acts as a magic spell that stops us from developing a massive ego.

Unfortunately, there's a trade-off. When you complain about your own inadequacies, you are actually being self-centered and, by extension, can come across as a tedious person with a sense of entitlement.

Do not subject everyone around you to a stream of unhelpful negativity that they don't want to hear. It's a waste of their precious time. They will resent you for taking up their energy.

Alternatively, we might think that minimizing our own accomplishments will stop other people becoming jealous, or even that it will protect us from bullying. Sadly, a lot of clever kids get bullied in school for being "nerds", and they learn to insult themselves first as a kind of protective mechanism.

If you were one of those kids, you may carry this behavior into the workplace and into your adult relationships.

2. Our parents or caregivers modeled the same behavior: A few days ago, I asked you to think about your personal communication history, and the messages you received from the people who raised you.

Children pick up their parents' habits. If they repeatedly undermined themselves, there's a good chance that you grew up thinking that this is a natural, normal way to behave.

3. We are so scared of failure that we'd rather preempt it by telling others how incompetent we are: If we tell everyone how unskilled and incompetent we are, they won't be surprised when we fail.

We don't have to deal with their disappointment, and we won't be expected to explain what went wrong. After all, they should have known that we wouldn't get very far.

At least, that's the logic we use. In a twisted kind of way, it makes sense. The problem is that this kind of talk can become a self-fulfilling prophecy. When someone tells us that we can't do something, we start to believe it. Ironically, by telling everyone that we are incompetent and that we are doomed to failure, we actually hurt our chances![45]

4. We have low self-esteem or even clinical depression: If you are plagued by negative thoughts about yourself, this could be a sign that you need professional help to raise your self-esteem or overcome depression.

It's worth making a doctor's appointment if you can't seem to find any enjoyment in life, or if you spend a lot of time feeling worthless, hopeless, or guilty.

Now, let's think about the consequences of self-deprecation:

---

[45] O'Banion, A. (2018). *Self-Fulfilling Prophecy – Breaking The Cycle*. Socialanxietyinstitute.org

1. You make yourself feel even worse: When you repeat the same message over and over again, even if you are alone, your brain starts believing it. A negative cycle is set into motion. You might even start beating yourself up for being so negative.

2. You miss out on valuable opportunities: Your closest friends will know whether your self-assessments are accurate, but new acquaintances and colleagues are forced to rely on how you present yourself when they form an impression of you.

If you tell them how lousy you are, and how all your achievements were matters of luck rather hard work and skill, they'll assume that it's true. They don't know your personal history, so what else are they supposed to think?

Needless to say, others will be hesitant to develop a relationship – especially in professional settings – with someone who doesn't have anything to offer.

Philosopher Mark D. White believes that a lot of us harbor a fantasy that "people will see through the self-deprecation to the person underneath." In this fantasy, we don't have to prove ourselves or be honest about our strengths and weaknesses.

If we wait long enough, someone will magically realize that we are actually a good, capable person. Writing in *Psychology Today,* White speculates that part of the problem is the fairytale narrative we were sold in childhood. Think of Cinderella – she got her happy ending when her prince looked beyond her meager home life and humble nature.[46]

3. Other people will assume that you are judging them: When you hear someone gossiping about an absent friend or acquaintance, do you ever suspect that they will start speaking badly of you once your back is turned?

This principle applies even if the person you are badmouthing is yourself. A steady stream of self-deprecating remarks sends a clear message – "I like judging people. I judge myself, and I may well be judging you, too!" Others will be slow to trust you.

---

[46] White, M.D. (2016). *Why You Might Want To Reconsider Putting Yourself Down.* psychologytoday.com

How to conquer the self-deprecation habit

The good news is that you can make a conscious decision to stop putting yourself down. In brief, you need to take two steps:

Step 1: Learn how to self-monitor and catch the comments before they come out of your mouth: I won't deny that this is difficult. If you've always been quick to point out your so-called deficiencies, you will struggle with this step.

I'm asking you to break the habit of a lifetime here. Be patient with yourself. When you catch yourself making a self- deprecating remark, just note it and move on.

Step 2: Change your thinking! Earlier in this section, I put together a list of the most common reasons why people put themselves down. Which example resonated most strongly with you? Dig a little deeper and get to the root of the problem.

You may need to address some of the unhelpful beliefs you are carrying around with you. For instance, if you believe that making self-deprecating remarks stops you from developing a big ego, remind yourself that lots of evidence exists to the contrary.

I bet you know at least one person who doesn't insult themselves yet remains grounded and realistic instead of big-headed. You can choose to model your approach to theirs.

Problem-solving can also empower you to change. Take an inventory of the things you dislike about yourself. If you can change them, put together an action plan and execute it. If you can't, it's time to work on self-acceptance.

No one is perfect and expecting yourself to be a complete success in every area of your life is a recipe for self-hatred and general disaster.

Put It Into Practice

Today, you're going to keep a running tally of how many times you put yourself down or belittle your own achievements when in conversation with someone else. You may be astonished by the end of the day when adding up the total.

Don't worry! I've worked with clients who made self-deprecating remarks over a dozen times every day. If they can change, so can you.

Tomorrow, aim to halve that number. The day after, make it your goal to make no self-deprecating remarks whatsoever.

Day 17: Ask Someone For Advice

We all love a story of a self-made man (or woman), but successful people often call on others for advice on their way to the top.

Asking advice from someone who has already been in your situation can save you a huge amount of time, because you will benefit from their experience and mistakes.

Not only that but asking for advice – if you do it in the right way – can also lead to good professional and personal relationships. People like to help, especially if they get the satisfaction of seeing their mentee or protégé succeed.

Think about it. I bet that when someone asks you for guidance, you feel valued. A sincere request sends a clear message – "I think you are exactly the right person to lend me the support I need, and I think it's worth making myself vulnerable if it means I get to hear your wisdom.".

Let's say you've found a person who is in a great position to offer you some valuable advice. For instance, they might be someone well-established in your field, or someone who has recently launched a successful venture. What should you bear in mind when reaching out?

1. Clarify your objective. What do you want to know? Before you pick up the phone or draft an e-mail, ask yourself about your end game. Imagine that you have already reached out for advice and received a response.

What would a good result look like? If you don't know, you need to think harder about what it is you want to achieve.

2. Give them some context. Don't embarrass yourself by diving straight in and asking for advice. Even if you are writing to someone who has a reputation for embracing questions and extending help to others, include a couple of lines that either remind them how and where you met or else let them know why you are writing to them rather than anyone else.

You should briefly explain why their advice would be relevant to your situation.

Entrepreneur Nick Reese, who receives hundreds of e-mails every month from business owners, states on his website that those who outline their personal problem are more likely to get a helpful response because he can tailor his answer to their question.

It sounds obvious, but apparently a lot of people don't appreciate how important it is to provide him with some background information.[47]

On the other hand, don't overload someone with information. Respect their time, and just tell them what they need to know.

3. Tell them what you want to achieve. It isn't enough to spell out your problem if you don't then say what you actually want to happen. For example, "I want to make a lot of money" is too general, whereas "My goal is to make at least $10K from my website this year" is much better.

This entails making your goals clear, which means making yourself vulnerable to criticism. There is a chance that you'll be told something you didn't want to hear. For example, let's say that you are looking to quit your job and start your own online business as an affiliate marketer.

Specifically, you want to be working full-time on your business within a year and generate at least $25K in the first 12 months. Your correspondent tells you that your goal is unrealistic and that it's more likely you will need to work on your site for a couple of years before quitting your job.

They tell you that if you can outsource some of your tasks and increase your advertising budget then you will make faster progress, but you don't have the resources in place. The feedback is disappointing, but at least you now have a realistic view of the situation and can adjust your goals accordingly.

---

[47] Reese, N. (n.d.) *The Secret Art Of Asking For Advice (& Mentorship)*. nicholasreese.com

I know, I know – it's awkward and painful to have someone tell you that your goals are unrealistic. But isn't it better to hear it straight now, rather than learning your lesson the hard way? Put your pride to one side and give them the full story.

4. Tell them what you've already done. In all likelihood, the person you are writing to has earned their success through hard work and initiative. They will have more respect for you if you tell them what you've already tried.

Be specific. "I've tried really hard and nothing's worked!" isn't informative. However, "I've invested $5,000 in PCC marketing, revamped my website two months ago, and used a 25-page e-book as a lead magnet but my mailing list only has 2,000 subscribers" provides a useful overview and proves that you aren't looking for a magic bullet.

In addition, never make the mistake of asking someone for help with a problem if you could just Google the answer.[48]

5. Give them a compliment. You can end with a brief acknowledgement of how their work has already helped you. It doesn't matter how well-established someone is, they usually appreciate positive feedback.

Don't overdo it. Something like, "By the way, I loved your recent article on putting together a marketing budget!" will do the trick. A bit of flattery can take you far but keep it sincere.

6. If you have mutual acquaintances, ask them for insight. Do you know someone who has already asked this person for advice or, even better, knows them personally?

If so, ask them whether there are any topics or questions you should avoid. If they have succeeded in getting advice from this person, how did they phrase their request? You could even ask to see any e-mails they sent, then use it as a template for your own message.

---

[48] Gervais, B. (n.d.) *7 Deadly Sins Millennials Make When Approaching Mentors*. americanexpress.com

7. Follow their lead when it comes to tone and message style. Take a look at your target's website or social media presence and use it to guide your writing style.

If they tend to use formal sentences and technical jargon, then a businesslike approach is best. If they are keen to portray themselves as a regular everyday guy or gal, then you will enjoy a better result by keeping your correspondence casual. If you aren't sure what they'd prefer, then err on the side of caution and use a conservative style.

8. If you are writing an e-mail, encourage them to follow up. If there is a chance that you will run into this person, perhaps at a conference or social occasion, tell them that you look forward to seeing them there. This makes it clear that you are keen to develop a relationship with them.

Of course, you should always send a polite note of thanks if they reply. Unless you have paid someone for a coaching service or they happen to be your boss, no one is obliged to give you any of their time. Always express your gratitude.

Put It Into Practice

Do you have a problem that drives you crazy? It can be personal or professional, large or small. Today, your task is to reach out to someone and ask for their advice. Remember, you don't have to take it on board if you don't think it will work. Your objective is to practice putting together a request and being brave enough to send it.

Day 18: Shut Down Nosy People

Human beings are curious by nature, but some people really take nosiness to the extreme. If you feel awkward when someone bombards you with inappropriate questions, today's exercise will be perfect for you.

I believe that most nosy people aren't even aware that they ask too many questions, or that their enquiries are about as welcome as wasps at a garden party. Fortunately, you can shut them down fast!

Here are a few ways to deflect someone who just won't take the hint. Obviously, you will need to pick the strategies that best suit your situation and the personality of the individual involved.

1. If you suspect they are bored, give them a task to do. Some nosy people aren't interested in your private life – they just want to break up the monotony of their day.

You *could* answer their intrusive questions about your weekend or whatever else it is that seems to fascinate them so much, but you could also try giving them something else to do.

Exclaim that you are so glad that they are free because your to-do list is so long. Tell them that you are busy and that perhaps they could lend you a helping hand? For instance, let's say you have a coworker with a habit of coming over to your desk and rambling on about nothing in particular. Here's how you could handle the situation:

COWORKER: Hi! How are you?

YOU: Ugh, I'm buried. Is there anything you need?

COWORKER: Not really. So how was your weekend? I went fishing. Caught a ten pound…

YOU: So, you've got a minute? That's great. Can I ask you to help me out with something? My to-do list is a mile long. Would you rather help out with photocopies or filing?

If you ask them for help every time they stop by "just for a chat," they'll soon get the message. Before using the above technique, make sure doing so won't put your position with the company in jeopardy. From an HR standpoint, there are situations where this technique would not be appropriate. For example, let's imagine the nosy co-worker is YOUR superior. You wouldn't ask your manager to run copies for you. Always utilize good common sense.

2. Flip it around. Although this isn't always the case, I've noticed that nosy people tend to love talking about themselves.

This is great news, because you can use the "flip it back" technique. All you have to do is give a non-committal answer to their nosy question, then turn it back on them.

In all likelihood, they'll promptly launch into a lengthy personal story. All you have to do is either pretend to listen or cut the conversation short and get on with your day.

If they don't want to share such personal details, they will be forced to acknowledge that their original question was inappropriate – if they don't want to answer it themselves, how can they reasonably expect someone else to respond? If they hesitate, you can say "Well it's a tough one, isn't it? Anyway..." and then shift the topic.

3. Bore them rigid. Perhaps a subtle approach isn't your style, and you want to use a bolder strategy? Try the "bore them rigid" technique. When you are asked an intrusive question, answer it – but in a really, really boring way that skips over the juiciest parts of a story.

For instance, let's imagine you've had a long day at work and you want to sit down with a nice glass of wine and read your mail. As you traipse out to the mailbox, your annoying neighbor asks a few awkward questions about your family life and presses you for the reason why you recently got divorced.

Rather than outline your spouse's affair with your best friend, you could give an intricate account of the nastiness of the rumor mill and how social media is ruining face to face communication.

Deliver all this information in a monotone without stopping for breath. If you pause, they will jump in and ask an inappropriate clarifying question. In short, you need to be seriously boring.

You may have to use this technique on a couple of occasions, but your nosy neighbor will quickly learn their inappropriate questions won't get answered.

A variation on this strategy is the "broken record technique." Give a brief answer, then repeat it until they get the hint and back off. Reveal no hint of frustration, but deliver the response in *exactly* the same way each time, using the same tone of voice and facial expression.

4. Say, "Why do you ask?" This question can disarm nosy people. It makes them pause, and the answer they give will reveal their real motive. They might have a good reason for making their enquiry, in which case you can answer the question.

On the other hand, they might scrabble around for a half-hearted response, which should make it plain to you and anyone else listening that they have no business sticking their nose in where it's not wanted.

5. Don't take it personally. Remember, nosy people are generally, well, nosy. It's unlikely that they are singling you out for special treatment.[49] Watch their interactions with their other coworkers or friends.

If you have a good relationship with their others in the same situation, you could even get together to swap strategies. You may gain fresh insight into the nosy person's psychology, and this will put you in a stronger position to deal with their behavior in the future.

---

[49] Green, A. (2014). *How to fend off nosy co-workers*. askamanager.org

6. If you have a good rapport, use gentle teasing or quips. Just because someone is nosy doesn't mean that they don't have a sense of humor. If possible, use this to your advantage. A remark such as, "You're far too nosy for your own good sometimes!" delivered with a smile and gentle laugh can be enough to draw a line under their question.

7. If a nosy person crosses the line into bullying, take it seriously. Nosiness is usually annoying rather than harmful, but occasionally it takes a more sinister turn. Anyone who uses invasive, inappropriate questions with the intention of making you feel uncomfortable, insecure or threatened is being a bully.

When challenged, they may contend that they just want to get to know you better, or even that they are trying to help you out. In this situation, you need to enforce your personal boundaries and let them know that their behavior will result in consequences.

The best tactic here will depend on the severity and context of the situation. Sometimes, all you need to do is tell someone that if they do not respect your privacy, you will leave the conversation.

It may be necessary to record their bullying behavior and then make a complaint to your company's HR department. Everyone has the right to go about their day without being subjected to scrutiny.

Put It Into Practice

If you come across a nosy person today, use the tips in this chapter and gently but firmly shut them down. If you escape all nosy people today, plan ahead for next time. We all have a nosy colleague, relative, neighbor, or acquaintance. Prepare yourself in advance, and you won't be at loss for what to say.

Day 19: Put Together A Persuasive Message

Do you work in a job that requires you to inspire, motivate, and instruct other people? Perhaps you just want to become more persuasive in general, or to dazzle people with your ability to put together a compelling message?

Some of us are born with the gift of persuasion, but don't worry if you weren't. We can all learn how to harness our inner motivational speaker. Today, you are going to practice using a tool that will make your speeches and everyday conversation more effective.

A few years ago, I came across a helpful technique that shows you how to do precisely that. It's called Monroe's Motivated Sequence, and it has a long and distinguished history. First developed by Alan H. Monroe at Purdue University in the 1930s, it's a template that will inspire any audience to take action. Obviously, you will need to tailor it to your specific situation, but the basic template will always be the same.[50]

I'll outline the steps, and then I'll provide a detailed example.

Step 1: Grab their attention Always open your argument with an emotive story, a shocking statistic, or a fact that will be new to the audience. A quotation or a rhetorical question will work too.

Step 2: Establish the need. Let your audience know why the current situation is unacceptable. Emphasize that things need to change, and fast!

Spell out the consequences – what will happen if no one takes action? In what ways does the problem affect your audience? You can throw in a couple of statistics here if they are relevant and interesting.

---

[50] MindTools. (n.d.) *Monroe's Motivated Sequence.* mindtools.com

Step 3: Tell them how you'll satisfy the need. Now that you've identified the problem, what's the solution? What options are available to you? What are the key principles underlying your approach? What, exactly, do you want the audience to do? If you have considered several options before settling on your preferred plan of action, explain how you arrived at the final decision. This kind of transparency will inspire trust.

Step 4: Paint a picture of the future. This step consists of two parts. First, you need to encourage the audience to imagine the consequences if they do not take action. Use emotive language but focus on facts and figures.

The second part is to share your vision of a brighter future. If the audience acts on your instructions, how will their lives improve? Don't be shy – spell it out! If you are giving a presentation with slides or handouts, include pictures or diagrams that will appeal to their emotions.

Step 5: Spell out the next steps. You should end by telling the audience what they can or should do next. After all, there's not much point in inflaming their enthusiasm without giving them further direction.

Here's an example of the sequence in action. Let's suppose that you have taken responsibility for the implementation of a workplace initiative.

This initiative has been set up to encourage people to increase their productivity. As their manager, increasing productivity 10% will be part of your performance assessment. You have been told to give a presentation to your colleagues, encouraging them to utilize some new techniques.

You could make the following points:

Step 1: Grab their attention. "Studies consistently show that a disturbingly high number of non-management employees could care less about their company's success and aren't working to their full capacity because of it."

Step 2: Establish the need. "If Corporate leadership expects non-management employees to be vigorously committed to the company's success, it's best not to neglect substantive incentives for lower-level employees."

Step 3: Tell them how you will satisfy the need.

Step 4: Paint a picture of the future. "As a result, management has decided to roll out weekly face to face check in meetings, no more than ten minutes in length to provide immediate and relevant performance feedback."

It's important to understand that the weekly meetings may not always provide positive feedback - that wouldn't be meaningful or effective - but that the communication will be thoughtful, accurate and relevant, regardless of the outcome. It could include encouragement for a job well done, or ideas and suggestions for course correction.

Step 5: Spell out the next steps. "Starting the first week of next month, your manager will schedule a standing meeting with you via your electronic calendar. If for some reason, you're not available, please work with your manager to re-schedule. All leadership will be receiving ongoing training for consistency across all divisions. Leadership will continue to meet at regular intervals to assess the effectiveness of the new program and also to review the productivity data."

If you need to improve your presentation skills, there's lots more advice on offer in my book *Communication Skills: A Practical Guide To Improving Your Social Intelligence, Presentation, Persuasion and Public Speaking*.

Put It Into Practice

If you work in a job that entails writing and giving presentations, you'll have plenty of opportunity to put this method to good use.

But what if you don't have to engage in much persuasion in the workplace? No problem!

This sequence – with a few minor adjustments – can work at home too. For example, let's say that you like the idea of buying a cabin in the mountains for vacations, but your spouse isn't keen.

You could grab their attention by showing them some photos of cabins (attention). Next, you could tell them that you need an economical solution for your vacation every year that also doubles as an investment (need) and that purchasing a cabin would be one such solution (satisfying the need).

You could help them imagine how much fun vacationing in the mountains will be (visualizing the future). Finally, you could then ask them to view a cabin with you (action).

Day 20: Improve Your Mediation Skills

Even the most non-confrontational people find themselves stuck in between two individuals from time to time. So, what should you do when faced with two warring colleagues, friends, or family members? In this section, you'll find a few useful tips that will help you defuse the situation while keeping everyone's dignity intact.

First, let's get clear on what it means to be a mediator. Whether it's a formal position at work, or a role you adopt in your social circle, a mediator's job is to act as an unbiased third party who helps two or more people sort out a conflict. The aim is to find an outcome that suits everyone – at least, as is reasonably possible.

Mediation is helpful when two people have tried to resolve their own problems but can't seem to arrive at a constructive solution. Don't confuse it with negotiation, which is a process by which the parties sit down and try to reach a solution together.

Here's how to mediate:[51]

Step 1: Make sure that you're a suitable candidate. Mediation should be voluntary for all parties, and a mediator should be as unbiased as possible. Furthermore, they should be capable of facilitating an exchange without imposing their opinion.

Does this sound like you? Be honest! If you have a stake in the outcome, or are biased towards one party, you shouldn't be acting as a mediator. There's good reason why organizations often call on the services of an external consultant when dealing with a dispute in the workplace – neutrality is key.

Step 2: Lay down the ground rules. A mediator is responsible for ensuring that discussions are carried out in a civilized manner. This means that everyone needs to follow an agreed set of guidelines.

---

[51] Skills You Need. (n.d.) *Mediation Skills.* skillsyouneed.com

As a general rule, the following are some good starting points:

-No one is allowed to speak over someone else;
-Everyone will get their chance to tell their side of the story;
-No one is allowed to bring up irrelevant issues;
-Everyone needs to actively engage with the process;
-All parties will focus on only one issue at a time;
-No one is allowed to verbally abuse, belittle, or harass anyone involved in the process;
-The main points of the conversation will be noted by the mediator, and copies will be made available to all parties following the meeting;
-Everything said in the mediation session will be kept strictly confidential, unless everyone agrees that the issue may be discussed elsewhere.

If you are mediating in a formal setting, you may wish to print the ground rules on a piece of paper and have everyone sign it as an indication that they understand how mediation works, and that they are willing to follow the rules.

You should also set out what will happen if someone violates these guidelines. For instance, if one party verbally abuses the other, the proceedings will be halted for ten minutes while both sides cool off.

Then, the offending party should issue an apology before the meeting continues. It's essential that you implement the rules as necessary, otherwise the injured party will lose faith in your ability to act as mediator. If you are intimidated by any of the personalities involved, you should not assume the role.

Step 3: Put together an agenda. Explain to everyone present that mediation gives everyone the chance to express their opinions, and that it's important that each side gets the opportunity to speak. Ask both sides – separately – what key issues they want to address during the process.

Encourage all parties to separate the facts from their emotions. For example, while someone may want to vent about the hurt that the other party has caused them, the underlying issue could perhaps be summarized as "Party X feels disrespected by Party Y."

You will need to draw on your best listening skills during this stage of the process. Unless everyone feels respected, the mediation won't be a success. Use active listening techniques such as paraphrasing and appropriate prompting. Paraphrasing is the act and process of restating or rewording. Appropriate prompting involves asking questions when you feel one or both of the parties are not being heard or understood.

Be sure to note down all the issues raised. The next step is to prioritize these issues so that they can discussed in a logical order. It's impossible to be prescriptive here, because every situation is unique.

However, the final agenda should make sense to everyone present. It should have some kind of "flow." For instance, you may all decide to tackle the most recent issue first, or you may wish to talk about them in chronological order.

Step 4: Listen to both sides so that you can understand the nature of the conflict. The next step is to move through the items on the agenda and invite each party to air their grievances. Take notes of the main points.

Ask individuals to repeat themselves if you lose track of what they said or if you require clarification. Quite often, someone who has become fixated on a particular issue or has become highly emotional will need more time than usual to gather their thoughts.

If one party feels intimidated by the other, you can suggest that each side be given the chance to speak with you separately. Remind everyone of the ground rules if necessary—everyone needs to stick to the facts wherever possible, and summarize their problems in an objective, calm manner. No one should be launching into angry tirades, and verbal aggression should not be tolerated.

In the event that physical violence erupts, the mediation process should be brought to a halt immediately. There is no excuse, under any circumstances, for physical abuse.

It definitely isn't your job to act as a bouncer or referee. Order the offending party to leave and call the police if necessary.

Step 5: Decide what issues need to be resolved. Put together a list of all details where the parties agree, together with their points of difference. Make this list as detailed as possible. When the parties can find some common ground, they are likely to approach mediation with renewed optimism.

Often, two people will enter mediation feeling somewhat hopeless. However, once they have calmed down and realize that they may have more in common with one another than they first suspected, this can break down a psychological barrier.

This phenomenon is frequently seen in child custody cases. Unfortunately, it is not unusual for parents to fight over child custody arrangements. Sometimes, a family lawyer will recommend mediation instead of a court case.

Trained mediators often encourage the parents to acknowledge their point of common agreement and interest – the well-being of their child. Despite their divorce and any grudges they may still hold against one another, most couples will agree that their primary objective is to provide the best possible life for their children.

Step 6: Oversee a brainstorming session. Your next task is to help everyone break the issues down into manageable chunks and to create a dynamic that encourages problem-solving rather than conflict.

Remind everyone present that they have some shared objectives – for a start, they both want to resolve the disagreement – and that they can take their time in coming up with solutions.

You can encourage everyone to brainstorm solutions as a group, or to come up with a list separately. You can then combine their ideas into one document, or pin them up side by side, and invite them to think about the pros and cons of each.

Remember, you must refrain from offering your opinion on which solution is "best." Your job is to ensure that both parties are given the chance to put forward their ideas and to encourage everyone to evaluate every potential solution.

Step 7: Encourage both sides to agree on practical goals. It may take some time – possibly a few hours, depending on the complexity of the situation and the personalities involved – but eventually, a few solutions will emerge.

The final step in the mediation process is to ensure that everyone sets sensible goals that can be reviewed later. Use the classic SMART acronym to help with this phase. Remember, goals should be Specific, Measurable, Achievable, Relevant, and Timely.

Invite the parties to draw up a written agreement and timeline for action, and then ask them to sign it. If one party refuses, it's time to take a step back and re-evaluate the solutions devised during Step 6.

Mediation does not always work. It requires everyone involved to take a mature approach to resolving disagreements. As you know, not everyone is capable of behaving like a reasonable adult. If your attempts at mediation fail, try not to take it personally.

Put It Into Practice

If you just so happen to come across a conflict at work or at home today, then go ahead and practice your mediation technique using the steps above.

If not, you can use the following exercise to see how the process works in real life. Think back to the last time you witnessed a heated argument or dispute. For example, perhaps two of your coworkers disagreed about the best way to proceed on a project, and neither wanted to back down.

If you could go back in time and act as mediator, how would the scenario have played out? Try to think of at least two possible solutions that the warring parties could have used.

Day 21: Drop The Clichés

We're going to round off this communication challenge with a simple rule that will immediately elevate you above other speakers. It's time to eradicate clichés from your everyday speech.

What's wrong with a cliché? In one sense, nothing. Popular phrases such as "smooth as silk," "Actions speak louder than words," "What doesn't kill you makes you stronger," "It's not rocket science!" "He's not a happy bunny," and "It's a big ask" aren't offensive. However, I'd still urge you to quit using them.

The trouble with clichés is that they have been used so often that they no longer provide the intended emphasis. Even if the cliché is literally true, it's just conversation filler.

Whoever you're speaking to will understand your meaning, but your message will lack impact. They've already heard the exact same words thousands of times before!

What's the answer? Get rid of them!

If you use a lot of clichés, you might notice a gap. What should you do instead? This is where you can have a bit of fun making up your own substitutes. For example, let's suppose that you are guilty of saying, "The grass is always greener on the other side."

You could experiment with the nouns and verbs to make your own version. For instance, you could try, "The apples always seem juicier the other side of the orchard, don't they?"

As you already know, a wide vocabulary makes you appear smart and engaging. Getting rid of the clichés automatically forces you to draw on a wider range of words, which in turn will give listeners the impression that you are an original thinker. If you can make up your own witty phrases and sayings, then so much the better!

These rules apply to written messages too. People skim over clichés. It's hard enough to get someone's attention these days, so don't lose them by stuffing your messages with overused metaphors or tired similes. Remove them entirely. This makes way for something more creative.

If you often use clichés in your speech, you might need some help in breaking the habit. We all have our own verbal tics, and our family and friends notice them more often than we do.

Be brave and ask someone you trust whether you fall back on the same old words and phrases. As long as you can convince them that you won't take offense, they are bound to have a couple of examples they can share.

Put It Into Practice

You have two exercises to complete today.

Exercise I

Monitor your speech for clichés. Try to catch yourself before you use one. If it's too late, make a note of what you could have said instead.

You can also watch out for clichés in other people's speech and writing. One piece of advice – don't point it out. They probably won't thank you for it.

Exercise II

Come up with three of your own cliché substitutes. Start by inventing your own version of "What doesn't kill you makes you stronger."

Personally, I prefer to say, "What doesn't knock you down only helps you stand firmer." The meaning is roughly the same, but it's a twist on the original phrase. When you use your own version, it grabs your listener's attention.

Conclusion

Congratulations! You've successfully completed the 21-day challenge, and your communication skills will be better than ever.

I hope you've had a lot of fun along the way and maybe even discovered something new about yourself. Other people will have started to notice the difference, too.

You should now be feeling inspired to take your communication skills to the next level – and I can show you how. I'm so passionate about helping people enjoy better communication in both their personal and professional lives that I've written several full-length books on the topic. They are packed with practical tips that will transform you.

Yes, it's a bold promise – but I stand by it! Once you've developed these skills, your relationships will become so much easier. You'll feel more confident, you'll enjoy a sense of control over your own life, and you'll start making plenty of new friends.

I've worked with hundreds of clients in my career as a coach and consultant, and I know that mastering new techniques saves careers, friendships, and even marriages!

One of the most rewarding aspects of my job is watching my clients learn these skills and see every area of their lives improve beyond their wildest expectations. Although I can't coach everyone who needs my help, I figured I could do the next best thing and condense everything I've learned into a series of books designed to let you realize your full potential.

Investing in your communication skills is one of the smartest choices you'll ever make. In doing so, you will set yourself up for years of career success, satisfying romantic relationships, and personal fulfilment.

Imagine having a professional HR coach in your back pocket or being able to consult a positive psychology expert whenever you come across a block in your personal life. When you buy my books, that's precisely what you get.

If you aren't sure where to begin, grab a copy of my guide to general communication skills. This will tell you everything you need to know about building great relationships. *Communication Skills: A Practical Guide To Improving Your Social Intelligence, Presentation, Persuasion and Public Speaking* is available in paperback, audio and Kindle editions via Amazon.

But wait – there's more! Once you've got the basics down, you can expand your communications toolbox even further with my latest book, *The Science of Effective Communication: Improve Your Social Skills and Small Talk, Develop Charisma and Learn How to Talk to Anyone.* It's full of no-nonsense tips on developing your charisma, making small talk, and building social confidence.

If you've ever felt socially awkward or hopelessly lost when trying to build relationships, this is the perfect book for you! Again, it's easy to find on Amazon and you can buy a copy in a format that fits your needs.

For those of you who want to develop advanced relationship skills – including skills that will make your romantic relationships so much easier – check out *The Science of Interpersonal Relations: A Practical Guide to Building Healthy Relationships, Improving Your Soft Skills and Learning Effective Communication*.
You'll discover why you keep repeating the same fights, how to rekindle the spark in your relationship, and so much more.

Finally, if you have a real appetite for self-help – and frankly, I can fully empathize with you on that front – I'd like to point you in the direction of my other books. Start with *Emotional Intelligence: A Practical Guide to Making Friends with Your Emotions and Raising Your EQ*, and *Empath: An Empowering Book for the Highly Sensitive Person*.

Check out my Amazon page for the full list and do stop by my website (mindfulnessforsuccess.com) to discover more about me and my work.

It doesn't matter whether you are a social butterfly, an introvert, or fall somewhere in between. If you put in the work, you'll see results. Anyone can learn to be a social success and enjoy all the benefits communication skills bring. May you reap the rewards of your efforts for many years to come!

One last thing before you go – Can I ask you a favor? I need your help! If you like this book, could you please share your experience on Amazon and write an honest review? It will be just one minute for you (I will be happy even with one sentence), but a GREAT help for me and definitely good Karma ☺. Since I'm not a well-established author and I don't have powerful people and big publishing companies supporting me, I read every single review and jump around with joy like a little kid every time my readers comment on my books and give me their honest feedback! If I inspired you in any way, please let me know. It will also help me get my books in front of more people looking for new ideas and useful knowledge.

If you did not enjoy the book or had a problem with it, please don't hesitate to contact me at contact@mindfulnessforsuccess.com **and tell me how I can improve it to provide more value and more knowledge to my readers.** I'm constantly working on my books to make them better and more helpful.
Thank you and good luck! I believe in you and I wish you all the best on your new journey!
Your friend,
Ian

My Free Gift to You – Get One of My Audiobooks For Free!

If you've never created an account on Audible (the biggest audiobook store in the world), **you can claim one free** audiobook **of mine**!

It's a simple process:

1. Pick one of my audiobooks on Audible:

http://www.audible.com/search?advsearchKeywords=Ian+Tuhovsky

2. Once you choose a book and open its detail page, click the orange button "Free with 30-Day Trial Membership."

3. Follow the instructions to create your account and download your first free audiobook.

Note that you are NOT obligated to continue after your free trial expires. You can cancel your free trial easily anytime and you won't be charged at all.

Also, if you haven't downloaded your free book already:
Discover How to Get Rid of Stress & Anxiety and Reach Inner Peace in 20 Days or Less!

To help speed up your personal transformation, I have prepared a special gift for you!
Download my full, 120-page e-book "Mindfulness Based Stress and Anxiety Management Tools" for free by clicking here.
Link:
tinyurl.com/mindfulnessgift

Hey there like-minded friends, let's get connected!

Don't hesitate to visit:
-My Blog: www.mindfulnessforsuccess.com
-My Facebook fanpage: https://www.facebook.com/mindfulnessforsuccess
-My Instagram profile: https://instagram.com/mindfulnessforsuccess
-My Amazon profile: amazon.com/author/iantuhovsky

Recommended Reading for You

If you are interested in Self-Development, Psychology, Emotional Intelligence, Social Dynamics, Soft Skills, Spirituality and related topics, you might be interested in previewing or downloading my other books:

Communication Skills Training: A Practical Guide to Improving Your Social Intelligence, Presentation, Persuasion and Public Speaking

Do You Know How To Communicate With People Effectively, Avoid Conflicts and Get What You Want From Life?

…It's not only about what you say, but also about WHEN, WHY and HOW you say it.

Do The Things You Usually Say Help You, Or Maybe Hold You Back?

Have you ever considered **how many times you intuitively felt that maybe you lost something important or crucial, simply because you unwittingly said or did something, which put somebody off?** Maybe it was a misfortunate word, bad formulation, inappropriate joke, forgotten name, huge misinterpretation, awkward conversation or a strange tone of your voice? Maybe you assumed that you knew exactly what a particular concept meant for another person and you stopped asking questions?

Maybe you could not listen carefully or could not stay silent for a moment? **How many times have you wanted to achieve something, negotiate better terms, or ask for a promotion and failed miserably?**

It's time to put that to an end with the help of this book.

Lack of communication skills is exactly what ruins most peoples' lives.

If you don't know how to communicate properly, you are going to have problems both in your intimate and family relationships.

You are going to be ineffective in work and business situations. It's going to be troublesome managing employees or getting what you want from your boss or your clients on a daily basis. Overall, **effective communication is like an engine oil which makes your life run smoothly, getting you wherever you want to be.** There are very few areas in life in which you can succeed in the long run without this crucial skill.

What Will You Learn With This Book?

-What Are The **Most Common Communication Obstacles** Between People And How To Avoid Them
-How To Express Anger And Avoid Conflicts
-What Are **The Most 8 Important Questions You Should Ask Yourself** If You Want To Be An Effective Communicator?
-**5 Most Basic and Crucial** Conversational Fixes
-How To Deal With Difficult and Toxic People
-Phrases to **Purge from Your Dictionary** (And What to Substitute Them With)
-The Subtle Art of **Giving and Receiving Feedback**
-Rapport, the **Art of Excellent Communication**
-How to Use Metaphors to **Communicate Better** And **Connect With People**
-What Metaprograms and Meta Models Are and How Exactly To Make Use of Them To **Become A Polished Communicator**
-How To Read Faces and **How to Effectively Predict Future Behaviors**
-How to Finally Start **Remembering Names**
-How to Have a Great Public Presentation
-How To Create Your Own **Unique Personality** in Business (and Everyday Life)
-Effective Networking

Direct link to Amazon Kindle Store:
https://tinyurl.com/IanCommSkillsKindle
Paperback version on Createspace:
http://tinyurl.com/iancommunicationpaperback

The Science of Effective Communication: Improve Your Social Skills and Small Talk, Develop Charisma and Learn How to Talk to Anyone

Discover the powerful way to transform your relationships with friends, loved ones, and even co-workers, with proven strategies that you can put to work immediately on improving the way you communicate with anyone in any environment.

From climbing the career ladder to making new friends, making the most of social situations, and even finding that special someone, communication is the powerful tool at your disposal to help you achieve the success you truly deserve.

In The Science of Effective Communication, you'll learn how to develop and polish that tool so that no matter who you are, where you go, or what you do, you'll make an impact on everyone you meet for all the right reasons.

Discover the Secrets Used By the World's Most Effective Communicators

We all know that one person who positively lights up any room they walk into, who seem to get on with everyone they meet and who lead a blessed life as a result.

Yet here's something you may not know:

Those people aren't blessed with a skill that is off-limits to the rest of us.

You too can learn the very same techniques used by everyone from Tony Robbins to Evan Carmichael to that one guy in your office who everyone loves and put them to work in getting what you want - without bulldozing over everyone in your path.

Step-by-Step Instructions to Supercharge Your Social Confidence

The Science of Effective Communication is a fascinating, practical guide to making communication your true super power, packed with expert advice and easy-to-follow instructions on how to:

- Retrain your brain to develop powerful listening skills that will help you build better relationships with anyone and gain more value from your conversations.
- Make your voice more attractive to potential romantic partners.
- Mend broken relationships with family members, partners, and even work colleagues.
- Get your views heard by those in authority without being disrespectful.
- Thrive in any job interview and get that dream job.

Your Complete Manual for Building Better Relationships With Everyone You Meet

Bursting with actionable steps you can use IMMEDIATELY to transform the way you communicate, this compelling, highly effective book serves as your comprehensive guide to better communication, revealing exclusive tips to help you:

- Overcome 'Outsider Syndrome,' make friends, and flourish in any social situation
- Keep conversations flowing with anyone
- Make long-distance relationships not only work, but positively prosper
- Reap huge rewards from a digital detox

And much, much more.

Direct Buy Link to Amazon Kindle Store:

http://getbook.at/EffectiveCommunication

Paperback version on CreateSpace:

http://getbook.at/EffectiveCommPaper

The Science of Interpersonal Relations: A Practical Guide to Building Healthy Relationships, Improving Your Soft Skills and Learning Effective Communication

From first dates and successful relationships to friends, colleagues, and new acquaintances, <u>unlock the hidden secrets to successful communication with anyone</u> and learn to flourish in any environment.

Guaranteed to change the way you think about relationships forever, <u>The Science of Interpersonal Relations</u> empowers you to identify those communication skills you need to work on and develop powerful techniques that will ensure your interpersonal relations thrive.

Your Complete Guide to Transforming Your Relationships

<u>The Science of Interpersonal Relations</u> is a book unlike any you've read before, not only in its approach to improving romantic relationships, but also on how to strengthen bonds and communicate better friends, family members, and even colleagues.

To really help you change your entire approach to communication, the book is split into two easy-to-read parts.

In part one, you'll change the way you think about the different relationships in your life and develop a whole new mindset that will lead you to healthy, positive, long-lasting relationships.

You'll discover:

- The real reason why so many relationships break down, and how to prevent yours from doing the same

- How to identify when you're being emotionally abused, and how to make it stop for good.

- Powerful solutions for dealing with negative people and protecting yourself against emotional vampires

- The secrets to successful assertiveness and the right way to say 'no' to anyone

- The links between personality styles and communication, and how to get the best out of any conversation with anyone.

In part two, you'll learn the tools and techniques you can put into action RIGHT NOW to start transforming your interpersonal relations for the better, including:

- Proven strategies for setting boundaries without hurting the other person

- The simple way for to help you meet your partner's real needs

- Effective techniques for identifying your partner's need for validation and providing it

and much more.

Discover the Real Reason You Don't Have the Relationship You Want - And What to Do About It

- Single and struggling to find that 'perfect' someone?

- In a relationship that you suspect might be in serious trouble?

- Dating someone you're convinced is 'The One' but not sure how to take that relationship to the next level?

Then this is the one book you can't live without.

Whatever situation you're in, single, dating, or struggling to keep that long-term relationship alive, you'll find simple-yet-effective instructions on how to create positive connections with the people in your life, including:
- How to determine what you really want in a relationship - and the red flags to watch out for that tell you someone really isn't right for you.
- How to turn heated arguments into positive experiences that help you and your loved one become closer and happier as a couple.
- How to identify if you're in a codependent relationship - and what to do about it.
- How to have "The Talk" about the state of your relationship and approach the subject of turning casual dating into something more serious.

Direct Buy Link to Amazon Kindle Store:
http://getbook.at/Relations
Paperback version on Createspace:
http://getbook.at/RelationsCS

Emotional Intelligence Training: A Practical Guide to Making Friends with Your Emotions and Raising Your EQ

Do you believe your life would be healthier, happier and even better, if you had more practical strategies to regulate your own emotions?
Most people agree with that.
Or, more importantly:
Do you believe you'd be healthier and happier if everyone who you live with had the strategies to regulate their emotions?

...Right?

The truth is not too many people actually realize what EQ is really all about and what causes its popularity to grow constantly.

Scientific research conducted by many American and European universities prove that the **"common" intelligence responses account for less than 20% of our life**

achievements and successes, while the other over 80% depends on emotional intelligence. To put it roughly: **either you are emotionally intelligent, or you're doomed to mediocrity, at best.**

As opposed to the popular image, emotionally intelligent people are not the ones who react impulsively and spontaneously, or who act lively and fiery in all types of social environments.

Emotionally intelligent people are open to new experiences, can show feelings adequate to the situation, either good or bad, and find it easy to socialize with other people and establish new contacts. They handle stress well, say "no" easily, realistically assess the achievements of themselves or others and are not afraid of constructive criticism and taking calculated risks.

They are the people of success. Unfortunately, this perfect model of an emotionally intelligent person is extremely rare in our modern times.

Sadly, nowadays, **the amount of emotional problems in the world is increasing at an alarming rate.** We are getting richer, but less and less happy. Depression, suicide, relationship breakdowns, loneliness of choice, fear of closeness, addictions—this is clear evidence that we are getting increasingly worse when it comes to dealing with our emotions.

Emotional intelligence is a SKILL, and can be learned through constant practice and training, just like riding a bike or swimming!

This book is stuffed with lots of effective exercises, helpful info and practical ideas.
Every chapter covers different areas of emotional intelligence and shows you, **step by step**, what exactly you can do to **develop your EQ** and become the **better version of yourself**.
I will show you how freeing yourself from the domination of left-sided brain thinking can contribute to your inner transformation—**the emotional revolution that will help you redefine who you are and what you really want from life!**

In This Book I'll Show You:

- What Is Emotional Intelligence and What Does EQ Consist of?
- How to **Observe and Express** Your Emotions
- How to **Release Negative Emotions** and **Empower the Positive Ones**
- How to Deal with Your **Internal Dialogues**
- How to **Deal with the Past**
- **How to Forgive** Yourself and How to Forgive Others
- How to Free Yourself from **Other People's Opinions and Judgments**
- What Are "Submodalities" and How Exactly You Can Use Them to **Empower Yourself** and **Get Rid of Stress**
- The Nine Things You Need to **Stop Doing to Yourself**
- How to Examine Your Thoughts
- **Internal Conflicts** Troubleshooting Technique
- The Lost Art of Asking Yourself the Right Questions and **Discovering Your True Self!**
- How to Create Rich Visualizations
- LOTS of practical exercises from the mighty arsenal of psychology, family therapy, NLP etc.
- **And many, many more!**

Direct Buy Link to Amazon Kindle Store:
https://tinyurl.com/IanEQTrainingKindle
Paperback version on Createspace: https://tinyurl.com/ianEQpaperback

Self-Discipline: Mental Toughness Mindset: Increase Your Grit and Focus to Become a Highly Productive (and Peaceful!) Person

This Mindset and Exercises Will Help You Build Everlasting Self-Discipline and Unbeatable Willpower

Imagine that you have this rare kind of power that enables you to maintain iron resolve, crystal clarity, and everyday focus to gradually realize all of your dreams by consistently ticking one goal after another off your to-do list.

Way too often, people and their minds don't really play in one team.

Wouldn't that be profoundly life-changing to utilize that power to make the best partners with your brain?

This rare kind of power is a mindset. The way you think, the way you perceive and handle both the world around you and your inner reality, will ultimately determine the quality of your life.

A single shift in your perception can trigger meaningful results.

Life can be tough. Whenever we turn, there are obstacles blocking our way. Some are caused by our environment, and some by ourselves. Yet, we all know people who are able to overcome them consistently, and, simply speaking, become successful. And stay there!

What really elevates a regular Joe or Jane to superhero status is the laser-sharp focus, perseverance, and the ability to keep on going when everyone else would have quit. I have, for a long time, studied the lives of the most disciplined people on this planet. In this book, you are going to learn their secrets.

No matter if your goals are financial, sport, relationship, or habit-changing oriented, this book covers it all.

Today, I want to share with you the science-based insights and field-tested methods that have helped me, my friends, and my clients change their lives and become real-life go-getters.

Here are some of the things you will learn from this book:

- **What the "positive thinking trap" means,** and how exactly should you use the power of positivity to actually help yourself instead of holding yourself back?
- What truly makes us happy and how does that relate to success? Is it money? Social position? Friends, family? Health? **No. There's actually something bigger, deeper, and much more fundamental behind our happiness.** You will be surprised to find out what the factor that ultimately drives us and keeps us going is, and this discovery can greatly improve your life.
- **Why our Western perception of both happiness and success are fundamentally wrong**, and how those misperceptions can kill your chances of succeeding?
- **Why relying on willpower and motivation is a very bad idea, and what to hold on to instead?** This is as important as using only the best gasoline in a top-grade sports car. Fill its engine with a moped fuel and keep the engine oil level low, and it won't get far. Your mind is this sports car engine. I will show you where to get this quality fuel from.
- **You will learn what the common denominator of the most successful and disciplined people on this planet is** – Navy SEALS and other special forces, Shaolin monks, top performing CEOs and Athletes, they, in fact, have a lot in common. I studied their lives for a long time, and now, it's time to share this knowledge with you.
- Why your entire life can be viewed as a piece of training, and **what are the rules of this training?**
- What the XX-th century Russian Nobel-Prize winner and long-forgotten genius Japanese psychotherapist **can teach you about the importance of your emotions and utilizing them correctly in your quest to becoming a self-disciplined and a peaceful person?**
- How modern science can help you **overcome temptation and empower your will**, and why following strict and inconvenient diets or regimens can actually help you achieve your goals in the end?
- How can you win by failing and **why giving up on some of your goals can actually be a good thing?**
- How do we often become **our own biggest enemies** in achieving our goals and how to finally change it?

• How to **maintain** your success once you achieve it?

Direct Buy Link to Amazon Kindle Store:
http://tinyurl.com/IanMentalToughness
Paperback version on Createspace: http://tinyurl.com/IanMTPaperback

Accelerated Learning: The Most Effective Techniques: How to Learn Fast, Improve Memory, Save Your Time and Be Successful

Unleash the awesome power of your brain to achieve your true potential, learn anything, and enjoy greater success than you ever thought possible.

Packed with proven methods that help you significantly improve your memory and develop simple-yet-powerful learning methods, Accelerated Learning: The Most Effective Techniques is the only brain training manual you'll ever need to master new skills, become an expert in any subject, and achieve your goals, whatever they may be.

Easy Step-by-Step Instructions Anyone Can Use Immediately

- Student preparing for crucial exams?

- Parent looking to better understand, encourage, and support your child's learning?

- Career professional hoping to develop new skills to land that dream job?

Whoever you are and whatever your reason for wanting to improve your memory, Accelerated Learning: The Most Effective Techniques will show you exactly how to do it with simple, actionable tasks that you can use to help you:

- Destroy your misconceptions that learning is difficult - leaving you free to fairly pursue your biggest passions.

- Stop procrastinating forever, eliminate distractions entirely, and supercharge your focus, no matter what the task at hand.

- Cut the amount of time it takes you to study effectively and enjoy more time away from your textbooks.

- Give yourself the best chance of success by creating your own optimal learning environment.

Everything you'll learn in this book can be implemented immediately regardless of your academic background, age, or circumstances, so no matter who you are, you can start changing your life for the better RIGHT NOW.

Take control of your future with life-changing learning skills.

Self-doubt is often one of the biggest barriers people face in realizing their full potential and enjoying true success.

In Accelerated Learning: The Most Effective Techniques, you'll not only find out how to overcome that self-doubt, but also how to thrive in any learning environment with scientifically-proven tools and techniques.

You'll also discover:
- How to use an ancient Roman method for flawless memorization of long speeches and complex information

- The secret to never forgetting anyone's name ever again.

- The easy way to learn an entirely new language, no matter how complex.

- The reason why flashcards, mind maps, and mnemonic devices haven't worked for you in the past - and how to change that.

- The simple speed-reading techniques you can use to absorb information faster.

- How to cut the amount of time it takes you to study effectively and enjoy more time away from your textbooks.

- The truth about binaural beats and whether they can help you focus.

- How to effectively cram any exam (in case of emergencies!).

And much more!

Direct Buy Link to Amazon Kindle Store:

http://getbook.at/AcceleratedLearning

Paperback version on Createspace:

http://getbook.at/AcceleratedLearningPaperback

Empath: An Empowering Book for the Highly Sensitive Person on Utilizing Your Unique Ability and Maximizing Your Human Potential

Have others ever told you to "stop being so sensitive?" Have you ever looked at other people and wondered how they manage to get through the day without noticing the suffering going on all around them?

Do you feel so emotionally delicate in comparison to your peers that you have tried to block out what is going on around you? You may have even resorted to coping mechanisms such as overeating, overworking, or smoking as a means of managing your emotions.

Maybe you have tried to "grow a thicker skin," or attempted to cover up your feelings with humor? Perhaps you have always felt different to others since childhood, but could never quite put your finger on why.

If this description resonates with you, congratulations! You may well be an Empath. **Unfortunately, an Empath who lacks insight into their own nature is likely to be miserable.**

Most of us are familiar with the concept of empathy. Aside from sociopaths, who are largely incapable of appreciating what another individual may be feeling, humans are generally able to understand what others are going through in most situations. Empaths, however, constitute the small group of people who not only understand the emotions of others, but literally feel them too.

In short, an Empath takes this common human ability of relating to other peoples' emotions to extremes.

If you have no idea why you are so readily affected by the emotions of others and the events around you, you will become psychologically unstable. You will be unsure as to where your true feelings end, and those of other people begin.

Hypersensitivity can be a burden if not properly managed, which is why it's so important that all Empaths learn to harness the special gift they have been given.
That's where this book comes in. Millions of other people around the world share your gifts and lead happy, fulfilling lives. Make no mistake – the world needs us.

It's time to learn how to put your rare gift to use, maximize your human potential, and thrive in life!

If you think you (or anyone around you) might be an Empath or the Highly Sensitive Person – this book is written for you.

What you will learn from this book:
- **What it really means to be an Empath** and the science behind the "Empath" and "the Highly Sensitive Person" classification. Find out how our brains work and why some people are way more sensitive than others.
- **What are the upsides of being an Empath** – find your strengths and thrive while making the most of your potential and providing value to this world (it NEEDS Empaths!) by making it a better place.
- **What are the usual problems that sensitive people struggle** with – overcome them by lessening the impact that other people's emotions and actions have on you, while still being truthful to your true nature, and learn how to take care of your mental health.
- **The great importance of becoming an emotionally intelligent person** – learn what EQ is and how you can actively develop it to become much more peaceful, effective, and a happy person. Discover the strategies that will help you stay balanced and be much more immune to the everyday struggles.
- **The workplace and career choices** – realize what you should be aware of and find how to make sure you don't stumble into the most common problems that sensitive people often fall prey to.
- **How to effectively handle conflicts, negative people, and toxic** relationships – since sensitive people are more much more immune to difficult relations and often become an easy target for those who tend to take advantage of others – it's time to put this to an end with this book.
- **How to deal with Empaths and Highly Sensitive People as a non-Empath** and what to focus on if you think that your kid might fall under this classification.
- **How to connect with other Empaths**, what is the importance of gender in this context, and how to stay in harmony with your environment – **you will learn all of this and more from this book!**

Direct Buy Link to Amazon Kindle Store:

http://tinyurl.com/IanEmpathKindle

Paperback version on Createspace:

http://tinyurl.com/IanEmpathPaperback

Confidence: Your Practical Training: How to Develop Healthy Self Esteem and Deep Self Confidence to Be Successful and Become True Friends with Yourself

Have you ever considered how many opportunities you have missed and how many chances you have wasted by lacking self-confidence when you need it most?

Have you ever given up on your plans, important goals, and dreams not because you just decided to focus on something else, but simply because you were too SCARED or hesitant to even start, or stick up to the plan and keep going?

Are you afraid of starting your own business or asking for a promotion? Petrified of public speaking, socializing, dating, taking up new hobbies, or going to job interviews?

Can you imagine how amazing and relieving it would feel to finally obtain all the self-esteem needed to accomplish things you've always wanted to achieve in your life?

Finally, have you ever found yourself in a situation where you simply couldn't understand **WHY you acted in a certain way**, or why you kept holding yourself back and feeling all the bad emotions, instead of just going for what's the most important to you?

Due to early social conditioning and many other influences, most people on this planet are already familiar with all these feelings.

WAY TOO FAMILIAR!

I know how it feels, too. I was in the same exact place.

And then, I found the way!
It's high time you did something about it too because, truth be told, self-confident people just have it way easier in every single aspect of life!

From becoming your own boss or succeeding in your career, through dating and socializing, to starting new hobbies, standing up for yourself or maybe finally packing your suitcase and going on this Asia trip you promised yourself decades ago… All too often, people fail in these quests as they aren't equipped with the natural and lasting self-confidence to deal with them in a proper way.

Confidence is not useful only in everyday life and casual situations. Do you really want to fulfill your wildest dreams, or do you just want to keep chatting about them with your friends, until one day you wake up as a grumpy, old, frustrated person?
Big achievements require brave and fearless actions. If you want to act bravely, you need to be confident.

Along with lots of useful, practical exercises, this book will provide you with plenty of new information that will help you understand what confidence problems really come down to. And this is the most important and the saddest part, because most people do not truly recognize the root problem, and that's why they get poor results.

Lack of self-confidence and problems with unhealthy self-esteem are usually the reason why smart, competent, and talented people never achieve a satisfying life; a life that should easily be possible for them.

In this book, you will read about:
-How, when, and why society robs us all of natural confidence and healthy self-esteem.
-What kind of social and psychological traps you need to avoid in order to feel much calmer, happier, and more confident.
-What "natural confidence" means and how it becomes natural.
-What "self-confidence" really is and what it definitely isn't (as opposed to what most people think!).
-How your mind hurts you when it really just wants to help you, and how to stop the process.
-What different kinds of fear we feel, where they come from, and how to defeat them.
-How to have a great relationship with yourself.
-How to use stress to boost your inner strength.
-Effective and ineffective ways of building healthy self-esteem.
-Why the relation between self-acceptance and stress is so crucial.
-How to stay confident in professional situations.
-How to protect your self-esteem when life brings you down, and how to deal with criticism and jealousy.
-How to use neuro-linguistic programming, imagination, visualizations, diary entries, and your five senses to re-program your subconscious and get rid of "mental viruses" and detrimental beliefs that actively destroy your natural confidence and healthy self-esteem.
Take the right action and start changing your life for the better today!

DOWNLOAD FOR FREE from Amazon Kindle Store:

https://tinyurl.com/IanConfidenceTraining

Paperback version on Createspace:

http://tinyurl.com/IanConfidencePaperbackV

Mindfulness: The Most Effective Techniques: Connect With Your Inner Self to Reach Your Goals Easily and Peacefully

Mindfulness is not about complicated and otherworldly woo-woo spiritual practices. It doesn't require you to be a part of any religion or a movement.

What mindfulness is about is living a good life (that's quite practical, right?), and this book is all about deepening your awareness, **getting to know yourself**, and developing attitudes and mental habits that will make you not only a successful and effective person in life, but a happy and wise one as well.

If you have ever wondered what the mysterious words "mindfulness" means and why would anyone bother, you have just found your (detailed) answer!

This book will provide you with actionable steps and valuable information, all in plain English, so all of your doubts will be soon gone.

In my experience, **nothing has proven as simple and yet effective and powerful as the daily practice of mindfulness.**

It has helped me become more decisive, disciplined, focused, calm, and just a happier person.

I can come as far as to say that mindfulness has transformed me into a success.

Now, it's your turn.

There's nothing to lose, and so much to win!

The payoff is nothing less than transforming your life into its true potential.

What you will learn from this book:

-What exactly does the word "mindfulness" mean, and why should it become an important word in your dictionary?

-How taking **as little as five minutes a day** to clear your mind might result in steering your life towards great success and becoming a much more fulfilled person? ...and **how the heck can you "clear your mind" exactly?**

-What are the **most interesting, effective, and not well-known mindfulness techniques for success** that I personally use to stay on the track and achieve my goals daily while feeling calm and relaxed?

-**Where to start** and how to slowly get into mindfulness to avoid unnecessary confusion?

-What are the **scientifically proven profits** of a daily mindfulness practice?

-**How to develop the so-called "Nonjudgmental Awareness"** to win with discouragement and negative thoughts, **stick to the practice** and keep becoming a more focused, calm, disciplined, and peaceful person on a daily basis?

-What are **the most common problems** experienced by practitioners of mindfulness and meditation, and how to overcome them?

-How to meditate and **just how easy** can it be?

-What are **the most common mistakes** people keep doing when trying to get into meditation and mindfulness? How to avoid them?

-**Real life tested steps** to apply mindfulness to everyday life to become happier and much more successful person?

-What is the relation between mindfulness and life success? How to use mindfulness to become much more effective in your life and achieve your goals much easier?

-**What to do in life** when just about everything seems to go wrong?

-How to become a **more patient and disciplined person**?

Stop existing and start living.
Start changing your life for the better today.

DOWNLOAD FOR FREE from Amazon Kindle Store:
myBook.to/IanMindfulnessGuide
Paperback version on Createspace:
http://tinyurl.com/IanMindfulnessGuide

Meditation for Beginners: How to Meditate (as an Ordinary Person!) to Relieve Stress and Be Successful

Meditation doesn't have to be about crystals, hypnotic folk music and incense sticks! **Forget about sitting in unnatural and uncomfortable positions while going, "Ommmmm...."** It is not necessarily a club full of yoga masters, Shaolin monks, hippies and new-agers.

It is a super useful and universal practice which can improve your overall brain performance and happiness. When meditating, you take a step back from actively thinking your thoughts, and instead see them for what they are. The reason why meditation is helpful in reducing stress and attaining peace is that it gives your over-active consciousness a break.

Just like your body needs it, your mind does too!

I give you the gift of peace that I was able to attain through present moment awareness.

Direct Buy Link to Amazon Kindle Store:

https://tinyurl.com/IanMeditationGuide

Paperback version on Createspace:

http://tinyurl.com/ianmeditationpaperback

Zen: Beginner's Guide: Happy, Peaceful and Focused Lifestyle for Everyone

Contrary to popular belief, Zen is not a discipline reserved for monks practicing Kung Fu. Although there is some truth to this idea, Zen is a practice that is applicable, useful and pragmatic for anyone to study regardless of what religion you follow (or don't follow).

Zen is the practice of studying your subconscious and **seeing your true nature.** The purpose of this work is to show you how to apply and utilize the teachings and essence of Zen in everyday life in the Western society. I'm not really an "absolute truth seeker" unworldly type of person—I just believe in practical plans and blueprints that actually help in living a better life. Of course I will tell you about the origin of Zen and the traditional ways of practicing it, but I will also show you my side of things, my personal point of view and translation of many Zen truths into a more "contemporary" and practical language.

It is a "modern Zen lifestyle" type of book.

What You Will Read About:

- Where Did Zen Come from? - A short history and explanation of Zen
- What Does Zen Teach? - The major teachings and precepts of Zen
- Various Zen meditation techniques that are applicable and practical for everyone!
- The Benefits of a Zen Lifestyle
- What Zen Buddhism is NOT?
- How to Slow Down and Start Enjoying Your Life
- How to Accept Everything and Lose Nothing
- Why Being Alone Can Be Beneficial
- Why Pleasure Is NOT Happiness
- Six Ways to Practically Let Go
- How to De-clutter Your Life and Live Simply
- "Mindfulness on Steroids"
- How to Take Care of Your Awareness and Focus
- Where to Start and How to Practice Zen as a Regular Person
- And many other interesting concepts...

I invite you to take this journey into the peaceful world of Zen Buddhism with me today!

Direct Buy Link to Amazon Kindle Store:

https://tinyurl.com/IanZenGuide

Paperback version on Createspace:

http://tinyurl.com/IanZenPaperbackV

Buddhism: Beginner's Guide: Bring Peace and Happiness to Your Everyday Life

Buddhism is one of the most practical and simple belief systems on this planet, and it has greatly helped me on my way to become a better person in every aspect possible. In this book I will show you what happened and how it was.

No matter if you are totally green when it comes to Buddha's teachings or maybe you have already heard something about them—this book will help you systematize your knowledge and will inspire you to learn more and to take steps to make your life positively better!

I invite you to take this beautiful journey into the graceful and meaningful world of Buddhism with me today!

Direct link to Amazon Kindle Store:
https://tinyurl.com/IanBuddhismGuide
Paperback version on Createspace:
http://tinyurl.com/ianbuddhismpaperback

About The Author

Author's blog: www.mindfulnessforsuccess.com
Author's Amazon profile: amazon.com/author/iantuhovsky
Instagram profile: https://instagram.com/mindfulnessforsuccess

Hi! I'm Ian...

. . . and I am interested in life. I am in the study of having an awesome and passionate life, which I believe is within the reach of practically everyone. I'm not a mentor or a guru. I'm just a guy who always knew there was more than we are told. I managed to turn my life around from way below my expectations to a really satisfying one, and now I want to share this fascinating journey with you so that you can do it, too.

I was born and raised somewhere in Eastern Europe, where Polar Bears eat people on the streets, we munch on snow instead of ice cream and there's only vodka instead of tap water, but since I make a living out of several different businesses, I move to a new country every couple of months. I also work as an HR consultant for various European companies.

I love self-development, traveling, recording music and providing value by helping others. I passionately read and write about social psychology, sociology, NLP, meditation, mindfulness, eastern philosophy, emotional intelligence, time management, communication skills and all of the topics related to conscious self-development and being the most awesome version of yourself.

Breathe. Relax. Feel that you're alive and smile. And never hesitate to contact me!

CPSIA information can be obtained
at www.ICGtesting.com
Printed in the USA
LVHW100056110719
623764LV00006B/19/P